AF798354

At a Glance

Curricular Goals Description	Competencies Description
CG-1: Explores and engages with the natural and socio-cultural environment in their surroundings	**C-1.1:** Observes and identifies the natural (insects, plants, birds, animals, geographical features, sun and moon, stars, planets, natural resources) and social (houses, relationships) components in their immediate environment **C-1.2:** Describes relationships (including between humans and animals/nature) and traditions (art forms, celebrations, festivals) in the family and community **C-1.3:** Asks questions and makes predictions about simple patterns (season change, food chain, phases of the moon, movement of stars and planets, shapes of trees, plants, leaves, and flowers, rituals, celebrations) observed in the immediate environment **C-1.4** Explains the functioning of local institutions (family, school, bank/post office, market, and panchayat) in different forms (story, drawing, tabulating data, reports), and analyses their roles **C-1.5:** Uses local materials to create simple objects (family tree, envelopes, origami animals) on their own for display or use in classroom processes
CG-2: Understands the interdependence in their environment through observation and experiences, developing the basis for appreciation of the idea of 'Vasudhaiva Kutumbakam'	**C-2.1:** Identifies natural and humanmade systems that support their lives (water supply, water cycle, river flow systems, seasons, life cycle of plants and animals, food, household items, transport, communication, electricity in the home) **C-2.3:** Connects changes in the environment and the lives of their family and community, as communicated by elders and through local stories (changes in occupation, food habits, resources, celebrations, communication)
CG-3: Explains how to ensure the safety of self and others in different (normal as well as emergency) situations	**C-3.1:** Describes the basic safety needs and protection (health and hygiene, food, water, shelter, precautions, awareness of emergency situations, abuse, and unsafe situations) of humans, birds, and animals **C-3.3:** Develops simple labels and slogans, and participates in roleplay on safety and protection in the local environment to be displayed/done in school and locality
CG-4: Develops sensitivity towards social and natural environment	**C-4.1:** Observes and describes diversity among plants, and birds and animals in their immediate environment (shape, sounds, food habits, growth, habitat) **C-4.4:** Demonstrates how natural resources can be shared, maintained, and conserved (trees, use of rainwater, benefits of millets) **C-4.5:** Identifies needs of plants, birds, and animals, and how they can be supported (water, soil, food, care) **C-4.7:** Learns about basic social and behavioural norms, values, and dispositions that benefit our social and natural environments and that help our society function smoothly (using dustbins, standing in queues, conserving water, using public transportation, keeping one's environment clean, always helping others in need regardless of background)
CG-5: Develops the ability to read and interpret simple maps	**C-5.2:** Draws a sketch of their school, village, and ward using symbols and directions **C-5.3:** Reads simple maps of city, state, and country to identify natural and humanmade features (well, lake, post office, school, hospital) with reference to symbols and directions
CG-6: Uses data and information from various sources to investigate questions related to their immediate environment	**C-6.1:** Performs simple inquiry related to specific questions independently or in groups **C-6.2:** Presents observations and findings through different creative modes (drawing, diagram, poem, play, skit, oral and written expression)
CG-7: Gains foundational familiarity with basic concepts and methods from the natural sciences (life sciences, physical sciences, and earth and space sciences) and engineering Understands	**C-7.1:** Gains familiarity with using the scientific method in investigations, as well as familiarity with other crosscutting concepts such as energy, matter, and systems that apply across the domains of science and engineering **C-7.2:** Gains familiarity with disciplinary core ideas in the natural sciences, as well as in engineering, technology, and applications of science, which reflect the content that will be learned across subject areas in later grades

Chapters	Curricular Goals	Competencies	Learning Outcomes
1. My Family	CG-1, CG-2, CG-4	C-1.2, C-1.4, C-2.3, C-4.5	**The learner:** • describes relationships within their family. • explains the role of family in one's life. • creates a simple family tree and uses it to explain a family structure. • identifies needs of different family members and how they can be cared for.
2. Going to the Mela	CG-1, CG-4, CG-6	C-1.4, C-1.5, C-4.7, C-6.2	**The learner:** • explains get-togethers as a time to meet family members. • describes various activities in a mela. • lists examples of melas held in India.
3. Celebrating Festivals	CG-1, CG-2, CG-6	C-1.5, C-2.3, C-6.2	**The learner:** • identifies the important days celebrated by the people of the country together. • lists the various regional, harvest and cultural festivals celebrated in India.
4. Games We Play	CG-6	C-6.1, C-6.2	**The learner:** • recognizes means of recreation and identifies indoor and outdoor games. • differentiates between objects and activities of present and past (at time of the elders). • identifies play and sports as work for some people.
5. Way of Life	CG-1, CG-6	C-1.2, C-6.2	**The learner:** • explains the different kinds of traditional clothes worn in various parts of India. • identifies the diversity in language and food of India. • describes the local games commonly played.
6. Plants around Us	CG-1, CG-4, CG-6, CG-7	C-1.1, C-1.5, C-4.1, C-6.2, C-7.2	**The learner:** • observes and identifies plants growing in the immediate environment. • classifies plants on the basis of shape, size and structure (flowers, fruits and seeds). • explains the process of germination. • describes what is a kitchen garden.
7. Animals around Us	CG-1, CG-3, CG-4, CG-6	C-1.1, C-1.5, C-3.1, C-4.1, C-4.4, C-6.2	**The learner:** • identifies simple features of animals in the immediate surroundings. • describes need of food for animals and their homes. • identifies insects and birds and labels their body parts.
8. Living in Harmony	CG-1, CG-6	C-1.3, C-6.1, C-6.2	**The learner:** • identifies ways in which plants, animals and humans depend on each other. • lists the uses of plants. • describes a food chain. • explains the ways to take care of plants and animals.
9. Water for Life	CG-2, CG-4, CG-6	C-2.1, C-4.4, C-6.1, C-6.2	**The learner:** • explains uses of water in daily life. • identifies the sources of water and ways in which it can be stored. • describes ways to save water.
10. Our Food	CG-2, CG-6	C-2.1, C-2.3, C-6.1, C-6.2	**The learner:** • describes the importance of food for good health. • explains the sources of food. • identifies the meals of the day and food requirements of different family members. • identifies healthy food and differentiates between fresh and rotten food. • lists the various regional dishes of India.

Chapters	Curricular Goals	Competencies	Learning Outcomes
11. Staying Healthy, Happy and Safe	CG-1, CG-3	C-1.5, C-3.1, C-3.2, C-3.3	**The learner:** • describes healthy practices for health and safety. • differentiates between good touch and bad touch. • discusses how to prepare for emergency situations like fire or injury. • explains the importance of happiness and well-being. • describes what is child labour.
12. Our World of Things	CG-6, CG-7	C-6.1, C-7.1, C-7.2	**The learner:** • classifies things around as transparent, translucent and opaque. • defines matter and lists the states of matter. • explains how matter changes its state from one form to another in various ways. • understands solubility and establishes why water is known as a universal solvent.
13. Things We Make and Do	CG-1, CG-4, CG-6	C-1.1, C-4.2, C-4.7, C-6.1, C-6.2	**The learner:** • identifies the types of houses and how they are built according to location. • describes how clothes are made and dyed. • explains how pottery was made by early humans. • describes the method of making pottery and cites everyday examples of use.
14. Mapping	CG-5	C-5.2, C-5.3	**The learner:** • understands what mental maps are and how directions play an important role in our lives. • explains the importance of maps and some of their elements. • draws and explains a sketch and line drawing of their school and neighbourhood. • reads a simple map with reference to some symbols and directions.
15. How We Travel and Communicate	CG-2, CG-6	C-2.1, C-6.1, C-6.2	**The learner:** • identifies and differentiates between the different modes of transport of the present and the past. • explains means of communication at home/school/neighbourhood. • describes occupations in transport and communication.
16. Managing Our Wastes	CG-4, CG-6	C-4.7, C-6.2	**The learner:** • observes and identifies the different kinds of waste that get generated in our homes and communities. • explains the importance of waste management. • describes ways of conserving resources and managing resources well in daily life to live wisely.

Contents

21st CENTURY SKILLS Observing

WHEN FESTIVALS COME

When Diwali comes, my sister Maya,
Will paint and light a big diya.
When Diwali comes, all good children
Get new toys and clothes in dozen.

I know my mother now will cook,
Sewians and gujias from her book.
While Dada comes and Dadi too,
Dadi in a saree and a woolly cap too!

I know its fun like August fifteen,
When we wore saffron, white and green.
All of which I think and dream,
Will be given when Christmas comes.
It's always fun when a festival comes.

Circle Time

1. In what way do we celebrate festivals with our extended family?
2. Name the three colours that would represent August 15. Why?
3. How do festivals help build culture and traditions of a place?
4. What are the different ways in which you celebrate festivals at home?
5. How do celebrations make you feel?

1 My Family

Learning Outcomes

The learner:

- describes relationships within their family.
- explains the role of family in one's life.
- creates a simple family tree and uses it to explain a family structure.
- identifies needs of different family members and how they can be cared for.

Warm-up

List the family members who live with you at home. Find out from your mother who taught you to do the following when you were growing up.

- Walk ____________
- Hold a spoon ____________
- Drink milk from a glass ____________
- Button a shirt ____________
- Tie shoe laces ____________
- Read and write ____________

C-1.2

We learn many things from the people who live with us. Our mother, father, brothers, sisters, grandparents, uncles, aunts and cousins are our family members. We love our family members and care for them.

TYPES OF FAMILIES

Some families are big and some are small. When only parents and their children live together in a family, it is known as a small or a nuclear family.

A nuclear family

When grandparents, parents and children live together, it is a big family. When parents, grandparents, children, uncles, aunts and cousins live together, it is known as a joint family.

In some families, children stay with only one parent, either the father or the mother. These are known as single-parent families.

People who are related to each other in a family are known as relatives. We know that the parents of our father and our mother are our grandparents.

Our father's parents are our **paternal** grandparents. Relatives from father's side are paternal relatives.

Our mother's parents are our **maternal** grandparents. Relatives from mother's side are maternal relatives. We are the grandchildren of our grandparents.

A big family

Extended Family

The brothers and sisters of our parents and grandparents form our extended family. The siblings of our parents are called our uncles and aunts. Their children are called our cousins. Siblings of our grandparents are called our grandaunt and granduncle. Their children are called our cousin uncles and cousin aunts.

Activity Corner

Find out from your parents the names of your grandparents' siblings and make a list of their names, their addresses and one special memory they have of spending time with them. If possible, look through family albums to get their photographs. C-2.3

A Family Tree

A family tree is a tree that shows how the members of a family are related to each other. All the people in the family who were born around the same time form a **generation**.

Your grandparents belong to one generation. Your parents, uncles and aunts belong to another generation. You, your siblings and cousins are all in the same generation. Your grandparents are two generations older than you, while your parents are one generation older to you.

In the family tree shown on the next page, the members of the same generation are in the same colour.

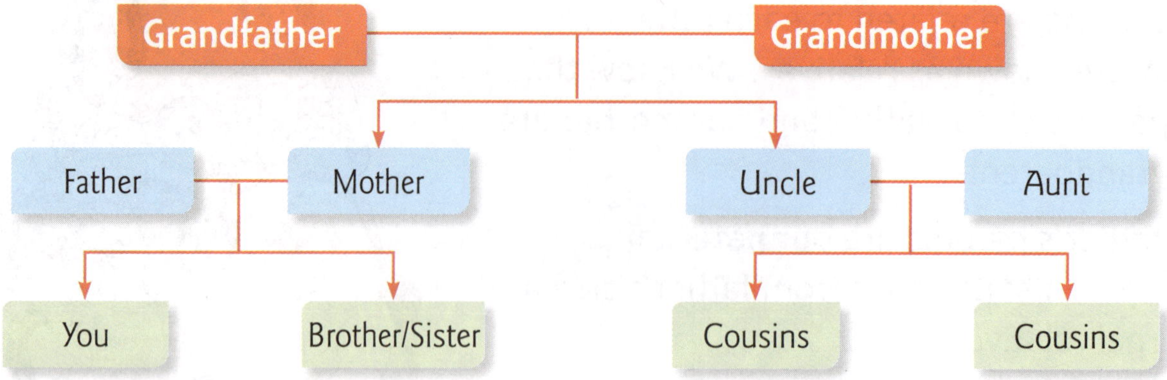

Living in the Family

We live with our parents, and sometimes with grandparents too. Everyone helps to keep the home happy. Parents work, cook, shop and care for us. Grandparents also help with chores and studies.

In Payal's home, her father cooks because her mother is busy. Everyone shares work.

Children can help by watering plants, dusting, and keeping things tidy. Families love and care for each other. We learn good habits and manners from them. We should respect and help our elders.

Payal's father cooking dinne

Sustainable Development Goals (SDGs)

Goal 12: Responsible Consumption and Production
As a family, a lot of wastes get created at home and many important things like water, food and electricity get wasted if we do not live wisely. As a family, we should try and reduce the wastes we produce and recycle and reuse as much as we can. Discuss and share how we can do so. C-4.5

SIMILARITIES IN A FAMILY

Write one way in which the grandmother and grandson in this picture look alike.

Do you look like anybody in your family? ___________

Family members are usually similar in two ways:

- In their appearance
- In their habits

A boy and his grandmother

Some family members may look similar to each other because they share certain **physical features**. For example, you may have hair like your grandmother and eyes like your grandfather, or a nose like your father and lips like your mother.

Fact Finder

When three children are born together at the same time to the same mother, they are called triplets (tri=three). Find out from your parents, if there are any twins or triplets in your family tree.

The features that are passed down from one generation to another are called **hereditary features.** Sometimes two children are born at the same time to the same mother. They are called **twins**. Twins may look alike. However, it is important to know that not all twins look alike.

Sometimes the members of a family may have similar habits. This is because they are related to each other and they learn their **values** and habits from one another. It is great fun to live in a family. A loving and caring family makes life **wonderful**.

My India

India has a very old way of keeping family records. Special priests called *pandas* write down names of family members, their births and marriages in big books called *vahis*. These books are kept safe in holy places and are updated when families visit. How would family records help the younger generation?

CARING FOR OLD AND ILL FAMILY MEMBERS

Sometimes we have family members who are ill and do not keep well. They need our special love and care. We can help them in many ways:

- We should give them clean and comfortable rooms.
- We should help them eat healthy food and get enough rest.
- We should help them get their medicines on time.
- We should try not to make noise around them.
- We should spend some time with them and keep them company.

We help old people in the family.

When people grow old, they may not be as strong and may need help. We should take care

My Eco Club

Plant a sapling with the help of your family. Water it regularly.

of them and their needs. Some elderly people live in old-age homes where they are looked after if they cannot stay with their families.

Be a Scientist

Make a list of all the different daily tasks that are done at home. Name the person who mostly does that task. Think and write how you can help in each.

Tasks at Home	Key Person Responsible	How I Can Help

Our Values

We should love and respect our family members. Each one is different and unique. Respect the uniqueness and accept each one as they are.

- Why is it important to give respect to our family members?
- How do you resolve conflicts with family members at home?

Let's Remember

Family

- Types of Families
  - Families are nuclear, joint and single-parent type.
  - A family tree shows how members are related to each other.
  - Family members help each other with housework.
- Similarities in a Family
  - We look like our family members due to hereditary features.
  - Members of a family have similar habits.
- Caring for Old and Ill Family Members
  - Sick people need our care and attention.
  - We must help the old people in the family.

New Words

Paternal: Related through the father's side of the family

Maternal: Related through the mother's side of the family

Generation: People in the family who were born around the same time

Physical features: Features of your body

Hereditary features: Features that are passed down from one generation to another

Twins: Two children who were born at the same time to the same mother

Exercises

A. Choose the correct answers. Remembering and Understanding

1. When we talk of one generation, which of these is correct?
   (a) Father, mother, grandfather, grandmother
   (b) Father, mother, uncle, aunt
   (c) Grandfather, grandmother, uncle, aunts
   (d) Cousins, uncles, aunts, grandfather
2. Which of these is true about paternal relatives?
   (a) They include all our father's relatives.
   (b) They include all our mother's relatives.
   (c) They are our mother's cousins.
   (d) They only include our father's parents.
3. Which of these is true about hereditary features?
   (a) They are passed down from one generation to another.
   (b) They make people have different appearances.
   (c) They make people have similar habits.
   (d) They do not occur in a family.
4. Read the statements below and choose the correct option.
   Statement (A): Parbeen has brown eyes like her father and paternal grandmother.
   Statement (B): Certain features are hereditary and can be passed from one generation to another.
   (a) Both (A) and (B) are true, and (B) is the correct explanation of (A).
   (b) Both (A) and (B) are true, but (B) is not the correct explanation of (A).
   (c) (A) is true but (B) is false.
   (d) (A) is false but (B) is true.

B. State whether true or false. Rewrite the false statements correctly.

1. Our Friends and family are considered family members
2. How we are related to each other can be seen in a family tree
3. We must help our family members at home
4. My father and grandfather belong to the same generation.
5. Your father and his sister are paternal siblings

C. Fill the crossword using the clues given below.

Down

1. People related to each other in a family are known as ________.
5. A family ________ shows how the members of a family are related to each other.

Across

2. We live together in a house as a ________.

3. A family where parents, grandparents, children, uncles, aunts and cousins live together is called a ________ family

4. Physical features that are passed down generations are called ________ features.

D. Answer the following questions.

1. Differentiate between maternal and paternal relatives.

2. What is a family tree?

3. List five ways in which you can help parents at home.

4. Why do family members look similar?

5. Give five things you would do to care for an old and ill family member at home.

Reflect and Learn

A. Discuss: There are special names by which some of us call our grandparents. Some common names are *dada*, *dadi*, *nana* and *nani*. What do you call your grandparents? Discuss and make a list of the new names that you may hear. Communication

B. Think and Answer: In the table below, add the names of the family members from the box in the correct spaces. Critical Thinking

	Generation 1	________________
	Generation 2	________________
	Generation 3	________________

Uncle Grandfather Cousin Aunt Brother Mother Grandmother Sister Father

C. Look at the picture and answer the questions:

1. Which type of family is shown here?

2. How many generations can you spot?

3. Make a family tree for the family shown.

Project and Portfolio

A. Individual activity: Pay close attention to the members of your family for a week. Identify one special habit of each and note it down. Do you see any similarities that run in the family? Draw them to make a chart. C-1.4 Creativity

B. Group activity: In groups of five, select any one family and collect information about the size and structure of the family. Draw the family tree with the help of a computer application and list the family values around the tree.

C-2.3 SI Computer Science

C. Interdisciplinary activity: In your scrapbook, paste or draw a picture of a recent get-together of your family. Also write four or five lines about it, in your mother tongue. SI Languages

D. Field trip: Visit an old age home nearby and read a story or play a game with the elderly. Spend time and find out a few problems they face in living there and make a short note. Suggest a few ways to solve the problems. C-2.3 Collaboration

Self-review

Colour the smileys to show how well you have understood the concepts.	Completely	Mostly	Need help
• I can describe relationships within my family.	☺	☺	☺
• I can explain the role of family in one's life.	☺	☺	☺
• I can create a simple family tree and use it to explain a family structure.	☺	☺	☺
• I can identify needs of different family members and how they can be cared for.	☺	☺	☺

Teacher's Tip

While starting the chapter, let the children talk a little about the family they live in. Try to engage the children who might be living with single parents. They should not be made to feel less fortunate. Discuss how some people who help us in school and home have left their families in villages and come to work for a living. Help children build empathy.

2 Going to the Mela

Learning Outcomes

The learner:
- explains get-togethers as a time to meet family members.
- describes various activities in a mela.
- lists examples of melas held in India.

Warm-up

Listen to the story *Idgah* by Munshi Premchand from your teacher. Discuss the following questions in class:

1. Where did the boys go in the story?
2. Have you ever been to a mela?
3. Write the main idea of the story.
4. Write down the similarities between the two characters, Hamid and *dadi* in the story.
5. What did you learn from Hamid, the boy?
6. If you had to rename the story, what title would you give?

C-4.7

GET-TOGETHERS IN A FAMILY

When we look at our families, we find that all the relatives in a family may not live together. They may stay in different places. We meet our extended relatives when there is a celebration in the family such as a wedding, a birthday or a festival. We also meet them during holidays and vacations. These family get-togethers teach us about our family values and also bring the family members closer.

We meet our extended family during weddings.

Sometimes families also meet and go together to recreational places like circus, magic shows, movie shows, **melas**, musical programmes, theatre, plays and sports events.

Make a list of the different places you've been with your family members:

(i) On a Holiday: ______________________________

(ii) For a Recreational Activity: ______________________________

Fact Finder

Some melas in India are so big that thousands of people visit them in one day! People come to shop, eat, watch shows and have lots of fun with their families.

GOING TO A MELA

Parzo and Meeta are going to a mela with their grandparents while visiting their *nani's* house. They are maternal cousins, and their mothers are sisters. Let us see what all they did.

It was a nice sunny, winter Sunday morning and the children woke up early to get ready for their outing. Parzo's maternal uncle and aunt were going to join them with their children. It was the Mela Day! Parzo and Meeta were excited. They put on their favourite clothes and got ready. Grandparents were busy packing some drinking water for everyone in clean water bottles.

'We are going to have so much fun!' squealed Meeta. Their mothers, uncle aunt and cousins were going to meet them at the mela ground.

Sustainable Development Goals (SDGs)

Goal 3 Good Health and Well-being

Going to a mela with family and friends makes people happy. Laughing, playing, and spending time together is good for our health and well-being! Have you been to a mela? Discuss your experience.

Parzo and Meeta tied their shoe laces themselves and held their grandparents hands and walked out. Since the mela ground was nearby, they decided to walk that short distance.

At the mela gate, the grandfather bought entry tickets for everyone and everyone waited for their relatives to join. The children had heard so much about this yearly mela and their eyes

Parzo and Meeta with their grandparents

sparkled to see the big open ground, colourful **stalls** and people selling toys, foods and little things near the entry gate. Excitement was everywhere.

Learning Corner

Draw three emojis in your notebook to show how you would feel going to a mela. If you were to go to a mela like this, who would you go with? Name five such family members and your relationship with each. C-6.2

A mela is a fun place where families meet or go together and plays an important role in our lives. It is not just a fun place, it plays many important roles:

- It brings together families and they spend time together.
- It keeps alive local **handicrafts** and food.
- People from different places of the country meet and celebrate together.
- It helps small artists show their crafts and sell them to make some money.
- It builds **culture** and **traditions**.

Be a Scientist

Make a mela **map**! Design your own mela ground with special places for the following:

- Any one food stall with your favourite mela food
- Your favourite mela ride
- Bins for trash

C-6.2

INSIDE A MELA

When we step inside a mela it looks like a fair full of fun, colour, games like darts and activities and people looking happy. People come with their families to enjoy rides like giant wheel and merry-go-round, buy toys like wooden toys and crafts, watch puppet shows, have delicious food like hot *samosas jalebis*, buy balloons and flutes and have fun together. There are dustbins to throw trash and to the mela ground clean.

Observe the picture of the mela on the next page closely and then complete the list by writing five things you see in each of the groups.

Games	Food Stalls	Toys	Handicraft Stalls	Fun Shows

My India

India has many exciting melas (fairs) that happen every year in different places. The Pushkar Camel Fair in Rajasthan is famous for camels and music. The Nauchandi Mela in Meerut has fun games and handmade things. The Kumbh Mela in Prayagraj is a very big spiritual fair held every 12 years. The Surajkund Mela in Haryana shows crafts made by people from all over India. How would a mela help people live better lives?

My Eco Club

We should not waste resources or throw wrappers, trash and bags on the ground in melas and other community events. They should all be thrown in a dustbin.

- What would you do with leftover water in bottles during melas?
- How can you reduce plastic wastes in melas?
- What would you do if you find wrappers and plastic bags lying on the mela ground? C-4.7

Festivals and Melas

Some melas also take place close to certain festivals. Teej is a common festival celebrated in North India, especially Rajasthan, during monsoons. Teej melas are popular among married women. Children's day is celebrated on 14th November every year. Many cities and towns have children's melas around that time, with lots of rides and fun activities, games etc. for children to enjoy. Diwali melas are also very commonly put up close to the festival of Diwali in many towns and cities. People meet, have fun, wear new clothes and meet each other at Diwali melas. Many stalls are put up where people shop and buy presents for Diwali.

Many melas are organized on Children's Day

Have you ever been to any of these melas with your family? ______________

Write any two special features of the mela you visited.

Our Values

Some melas are held to help people in need. Part of the money from things sold is given to help others. For example, the Blind School in Delhi has a big mela every year before Diwali to raise money for visually disabled people.

- How can we help in these melas?
- Do you think it is a good idea to buy things in these melas? Why?

Let's Remember

Going to the Mela

- **Get-togethers in a Family** → We meet our extended family on occasions like weddings, birthdays and festivals.
- **Going to a Mela** → A mela is a fun place. It brings families together, keeps alive local handicrafts and food, and builds culture and traditions.
- **Inside a Mela** →
  - A mela has many attractions like cultural shows and fun rides, local food and handicrafts as well as games.
  - Melas also take place during many festivals like Teej, Diwali and Children's Day.

New Words

Mela: A fun place that has a variety of temporary shops called stalls

Stall: A temporary enclosed area used as a shop for a short time

Handicraft: Craft articles made by craftsmen using traditional methods by hand

Culture: The customs and beliefs, art, way of life and social structure of a particular country or group

Tradition: A belief, custom or way of doing something that has existed for a long time among a particular group of people

Map: A sketch or a drawing of a place

Exercises

Remembering and Understanding

A. Choose the correct answers.

1. When do we usually meet our extended family members?
   (a) Vacations (b) Holidays (c) Festivals (d) All of these
2. Which of these is not a place for families to meet for fun?
   (a) Sports event (b) Mela (c) Movie shows (d) Bank
3. What did Parzo and Meeta's grandfather buy at the mela gate?
   (a) Jalebis (b) Tickets (c) Wooden toys (d) Bangles
4. Read the statements below and choose the correct option.
   Statement (A): A mela is a fun place we go with family.
   Statement (B): A mela has many stalls and rides, something for everyone in the family.

(a) Both (A) and (B) are true, and (B) is the correct explanation of (A).

(b) Both (A) and (B) are true, but (B) is not the correct explanation of (A).

(c) (A) is true but (B) is false. (d) (A) is false but (B) is true.

B. Match the following to which section you would go for each of these in a mela.

1. Food stall	2. Game stall	3. Rides	4. Show corner	5. Handicrafts
(a) Wooden toys	(b) Hot *jalebis*	(c) Puppet show	(d) Giant wheel	(e) Darts

C. Fill in the Blanks.

1. We meet our relatives when there is a ________________ in the family such as a wedding or a festival. (celebration/mela)
2. Family get-togethers teach us about our family ________________. (values/numbers)
3. A mela is a ________________ (vacation /fun) place where families meet or go together and plays an important role in our lives.
4. We find ________________ (stalls/rides) in a mela.
5. There are ________________ (dustbins/rides) to throw trash and keep the mela ground clean.

D. Answer the following questions.

1. Mention any three celebrations when we usually meet our extended family.
2. Name any three family get-togethers that families go to for fun.
3. List any three kinds of stalls one can find in a mela.
4. What are five ways in which a mela plays an important role?
5. Why are melas important for small artists and sellers?
6. How can we keep a melaground clean?
7. Name any three festivals around which we find melas in our city.

Reflect and Learn

21st CENTURY SKILLS

A. Discuss: How can we show respect and care for others at the mela? Communication

B. Think and Answer: Why are melas held in open spaces? Do you think a mela is a fun place that preserves the traditions and culture? Critical Thinking

C. Look at the picture on the next page and answer the questions:

1. What is shown here?
2. List all the activities happening in your notebook.

Project and Portfolio

A. Individual activity: If you had to become a Hero and design a Green Mela, what changes would you suggest? Create a set of rules and special features for the mela. Also make a poster to promote responsible use and less waste. C-4.7 Creativity

B. Group activity: In your group of three, make a giant wheel for a mela using straws and play dough. Work together and have fun building it. After you finish, talk about two things that were a bit tough and how your group worked together to fix them. C-1.5 Collaboration

C. Interdisciplinary activity: Write an imaginary and descriptive account of a day you spent with your cousins on a mela. Draw a picture to show the mela set up and what kind of stalls the mela had, and the fun you had. C-1.4 SI Arts Education

Self-review

Colour the smileys to show how well you have understood the concepts.	Completely	Mostly	Need help
• I can explain get-togethers as a time to meet family members.	☺	☺	☺
• I can describe various activities in a mela.	☺	☺	☺
• I can list examples of melas held in India.	☺	☺	☺

Teacher's Tip

Encourage the learners to find out more about melas held in their village, town or city.

3 Celebrating Festivals

Learning Outcomes

The learner:
- identifies the important days celebrated by the people of the country together.
- lists the various regional, harvest and cultural festivals celebrated in India.

Warm-up

Play the game of passing the parcel where children sit in a circle and pass a small bag with chits that have word clues related to religious festivals, harvest festivals and important days we have already studied in earlier classes.

Once music starts, everyone passes the bag. When the music stops, whoever has the bag takes out a chit and guesses the festival, based on a word clue.

WE CELEBRATE FESTIVALS TOGETHER

We celebrate many festivals in India. Festivals help to bring people together and help live with each other in harmony. Festivals also help to keep the culture and traditions alive and make bonds of **communities** stronger. They also help some people earn money, as we buy new clothes, presents and sweets etc. However, festival time can also generate a lot of wastes and lead to a lot of wastage of resources. We should celebrate festivals wisely.

Sustainable Development Goals (SDGs)

Goal 12: Responsible Consumption and Production

During festivals, people enjoy food, decorations and celebrations. But sometimes, too much waste is created from plastic plates, leftover food and decorations. What can we do during festivals to help keep the environment clean?

Though many religious and other festivals are celebrated by everyone all across India, there are some that are celebrated more **locally** in specific regions. They are known as regional festivals.

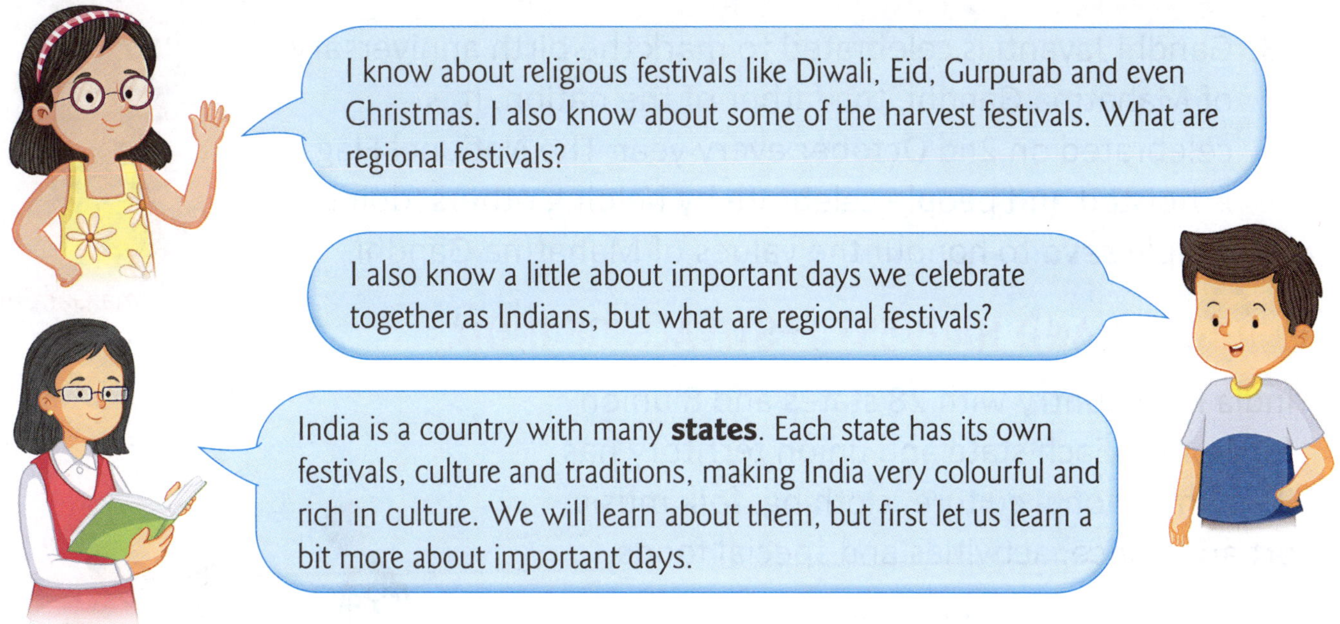

IMPORTANT DAYS

We celebrate many important days as people of the country. They involve hoisting the National Flag and singing the National Anthem. All national days are holidays for the entire country. Each person in the country celebrates these festivals, no matter what religion they follow or the region they live in.

Fact Finder

The National Anthem of India was written by Rabindranath Tagore.

In India, we celebrate mainly three such important days:

People celebrate Independence Day on 15th August.

1. Independence Day on the 15th August marks the day India got freedom from the British. The Prime minister of India hoists the National Flag on the Red Fort in Delhi on this day.
2. Republic Day is celebrated on 26th January every year to mark the day when India became a Republic in 1950. On this day, the President of India hoists the National Flag. There is a parade called the Republic Day parade, which showcases the power of India in all spheres, on the Rajpath, now known as the Kartavya Path in New Delhi on this day. Many **tableaux** showcase the culture and traditions of each state of India during the Republic Day Parade.

3. Gandhi Jayanti is celebrated to mark the birth anniversary of Mahatma Gandhi, the father of the nation. It is celebrated on 2nd October every year. The National Flag is hoisted and people celebrate by helping others, doing simple ***seva*** to honour the values of Mahatma Gandhi.

Mahatma Gandhi

REGIONAL AND HARVEST FESTIVALS OF INDIA

India is a country with 28 states and 8 union territories. Each state and union territory has its own regional culture, clothing, **folk** music, art and dance, activities and special foods.

A family celebrating Gudi Padwa

Let us look at some popular regional and harvest festivals celebrated in different regions and states.

Ganesh Utsav and Gudi Padwa are important festivals celebrated in Maharashtra. Ganesh Utsav is a ten-day festival of celebrating the birth of Ganesh, the elephant faced Hindu god. *Modak* is a special sweet dish made on Ganesh Utsav. Gudi Padwa is celebrated as the Hindu New Year in Maharashtra. People make rangoli designs at the entrance of their homes and decorate it with flowers. Special sweets of this festival are Shrikhand, Puran Poli and Sunth Paak.

Puran Poli

Chhath Puja is a very popular festival in Bihar, where people worship the sun god, while observing fast and staying in the river the entire night to offer water and other offerings to the sun god at sunrise. People make a traditional sweet called thekua and other foods like *kaddu bhaat* (pumpkin curry with rice), *rasiyaw* (a type of kheer) and *dahi chuda*.

Pongal dish

Ugadi is a harvest festival in Andhra Pradesh, Karnataka, and Telangana. This harvest festival is observed by making rangolis on the floor, decorations on doors called toran, buying and giving gifts and sharing special food like tamarind rice. It is also celebrated as the Hindu New Year.

Pongal is celebrated not just in Tamil Nadu but also other regions of South India. Pongal rice is the traditional food of this festival and the houses are decorated by traditional floral designs using rice, coloured powders and flower petals.

Bihu is the popular festival of Assam, one of the North Eastern states of India. People wear traditional clothes and perform the traditional Bihu dance in their fields and homes as part of their celebrations.

Activity Corner

Study and complete rangoli the design.

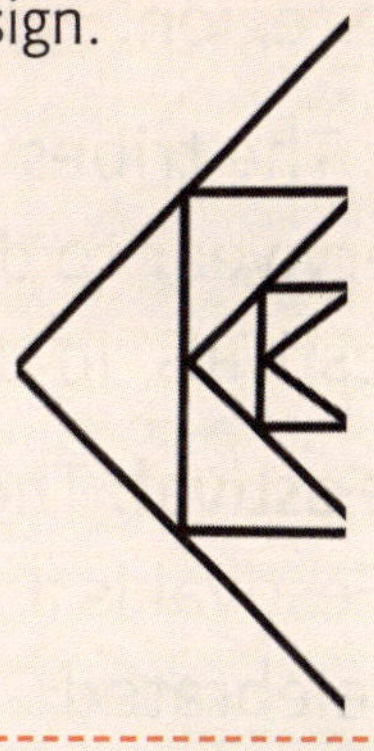

My Eco Club

Pongal is traditionally served on a banana leaf. This practice is not only cultural but also eco-friendly.

Baisakhi is the harvest festival of Punjab. Local folk dances like giddha and bhangra are specially performed by people in traditional clothes during this festival

Teej and Gangaur are famous festivals in Rajasthan that people celebrate in a local way, special to their own towns and villages. They are festivals to honour and celebrate women where they get mehendi put on their hands and get presents from families. *Ghewar* and *Phirni* are traditional sweets eaten.

Mehendi design on hand

Durga Puja is celebrated in Bengal with big pandals and ten-armed Goddess Durga idols. In many cities, there is mela like environment and decorative areas called *pandals* are set up, where people go and enjoy the music, food, clothing and religious activities during Navratras.

My India

Hemis, is a two-day religious festival celebrated mostly in Ladakh and Jammu Kashmir. In this festival, Buddhist priests perform a special Cham dance with the traditional music of cymbals, drums and even trumpets played by the monks. The priests and monks who dance, wear masks and fancy clothes. Do you think music, dance and masks can help in expressing feelings?

CULTURAL FESTIVALS

Some regions in India also celebrate special yearly festivals to show the culture and beauty of the region.

Hornbill Festival: The tribes of Nagaland celebrate this festival in the first week of December every year to display their culture. This festival is also known as the 'Festival of Festivals' in that region.

Cherry Blossom Festival: The Cherry Blossom Festival is a cultural festival celebrated yearly in November in Shillong, Meghalaya. It is celebrated to showcase the beauty of the Himalayan cherry blossoms, that bloom at that time. Many cultural events are also held as part of the festival.

Cherry blossoms

Tulip Festival: Jammu and Kashmir celebrates the Tulip festival yearly in the month of April to celebrate the blooming of tulips in the Tulip Gardens of Srinagar. This festival showcases the beauty of tulips an-d draws many people to Srinagar.

Changes in Local Celebrations

Over time, how people celebrate local festivals has undergone a lot of change. The migration of people from their original places, the levels of education and influence of other cultures have played a major role in the way people celebrate festivals. Many rituals have been simplified or even overlooked.

Our Values

When we celebrate festivals, a lot of waste gets collected. We should we wise in how we manage those wastes. When we immerse idols and throw used flowers and other things in water bodies, we harm them.

- How can we prevent harming water bodies by making wiser choices during festivals?

Let's Remember

Celebrating Festivals

- **We Celebrate Festivals Together** → Festivals bring families and communities closer to each other.
- **Important Days** → We celebrate important days together as a country, such as Republic Day and Independence Day.
- **Regional and Harvest Festivals of India** → Festivals such as Ganesh Chaturthi and Chhath Puja are celebrated in certain regions. Festivals like Pongal and Baisakhi are harvest festivals.
- **Cultural Festivals** → Some regions in India also celebrate special yearly festivals to showcase the culture and beauty of the region.

New Words

Community: A group of people who live, work, or play together and help each other.
Local: Belonging to or connected with the particular place or area that you are talking about or with the place where you live
State: A defined geographical area with recognized borders.
Tableaux: A grouping or arrangement to represent something visually
Seva: Helping others without expecting anything in return
Folk: The local people in a country or community and their old customs, songs, and stories.

Exercises

A. Choose the correct answers. Remembering and Understanding

1. We celebrate _______ festivals in India.
   (a) less (b) many (c) few (d) zero
2. Which of the following is an important day?
   (a) Gudi padwa (b) Baisakhi (c) Independence Day (d) Teej
3. In which of the following states is Bihu celebrated?
   (a) Punjab (b) Assam (c) Nagaland (d) Meghalaya
4. The tribes of Nagaland celebrate which of the following festivals?
   (a) Canary (b) Parrot (c) Robin (d) Hornbill

5. Read the statements below and choose the correct option.
Statement (A): Baisakhi is celebrated mainly in Punjab.
Statement (B): Farming is popular in Punjab and Baisakhi is a harvest festival.
(a) Both (A) and (B) are true, and (B) is the correct explanation of (A).
(b) Both (A) and (B) are true, but (B) is not the correct explanation of (A).
(c) (A) is true but (B) is false. (d) (A) is false but (B) is true.

B. Match the rows.

1. Gudi Padwa	2. Pongal	3. Baisakhi	4. Gangaur	5. Cherry Blossom
(a) Punjab	(b) Maharashtra	(c) Tamil Nadu	(d) Shillong	(e) Rajasthan

C. Name the following.

1. The important day on which India got independence: ________________
2. Popular festival of Assam: ________________
3. The dish prepared during Ugadi: ________________
4. The festival in which people perform Bhangra: ________________
5. The decorative areas during Durga Puja: ________________

D. Answer the following questions.

1. How do festivals help us?
2. Mention two ways in which festivals can harm the environment.
3. In what ways is Independence Day different to the Republic Day?
4. How many states and union territories form India?
5. What are cultural festivals? Give two examples.
6. How have local celebrations changed over time?

Reflect and Learn

21st CENTURY SKILLS

A. Discuss: Name any one regional festival that is celebrated at home. Find out the traditional sweet dish that is made during that festival, and the local folklore around that festival, from elders in your family. Share in class. Communication

B. Think and Answer: How do festivals help in bringing people together? Critical Thinking

C. Read the text and answer the questions: India celebrates many harvest festivals. These festivals happen when crops are ready to be picked. In Punjab, people celebrate Lohri with songs and dancing around a fire. In Tamil Nadu, Pongal is celebrated by cooking sweet rice. In Assam, Bihu is a happy time with music and games.
1. Why do people celebrate harvest festivals?
2. Name one harvest festival from Tamil Nadu.
3. How do people in Punjab celebrate Lohri?

D. Look at the picture and answer the questions:

1. Identify the flowers.
2. Which festival are they associated with?
3. Where is this festival celebrated?
4. Write one feature of this festival.

Project and Portfolio

A. Individual activity: With help from your parents, find one religious, one harvest, and one regional festival your family celebrates. Learn how and why each is celebrated, and what your family does to get ready—like cooking special food or decorating the house. Make a flipbook to show these festivals. You can use old calendar pages and tie them together with thread. Try to reuse paper! C-6.2 Creativity

B. Group activity: In groups of five, visit a local shop with an elder. Make a list of ten questions to find out: how festivals help them increase their earnings; what preparations do they do for the upcoming festivals; How do festivals help in improving their lives. In groups make a chart to show all the information collected and then talk about it in class. C-2.3 SI Mathematics Collaboration

C. Interdisciplinary activity: In groups of five, collect powdered rice or coloured powders and flower petals. Decide on a geometrical design that includes a minimum of 6 circles, 6 squares, 6 triangles and 6 hearts. Now in groups, make this rangoli on the floor and show your teacher. C-1.5 Creativity and Collaboration

Self-review

Colour the smileys to show how well you have understood the concepts.	Completely	Mostly	Need help
• I can identify the important days celebrated by the people of the country together.	☺	☺	☺
• I can list the various regional, harvest and cultural festivals celebrated in India.	☺	☺	☺

Teacher's Tip

Start the lesson by asking children to talk about the festivals they celebrate with family and friends. Discuss some festivals they may not know about. This helps them learn how festivals are different in each place and why they are important.

4 Games We Play

Learning Outcomes

The learner:

- recognizes means of recreation and identifies indoor and outdoor games.
- differentiates between objects and activities of present and past (at time of the elders).
- identifies play and sports as work for some people.

Warm-up

Make a list of the games you like playing with each of the following:

1. Your friends in school ____________________
2. Your friends after school ____________________
3. Your siblings ____________________
4. Your cousins ____________________
5. Your parents ____________________
   - Out of these, which is your favourite game? Circle it.
   - How does playing that game make you feel? Write three words to describe your feelings ____________________

C-6.2

There are many things that we like to do in our free time. We like reading, painting, watching television, listening to music, cycling, playing and doing many other things.

The free time when we do things that we enjoy is known as leisure or recreation. The things that we like to do in our spare time are called means of recreation. We feel fresh, relaxed and happy after we do these things.

Asha likes to listen to music.

What do you like to do in your free time? ____________________________

I have seen people playing games in their free time.

Yes. People like to play different games in their free time. Let us learn about them

Sustainable Development Goals (SDGs)

Goal 3: Good Health and Well-being

Some games are known to help us in releasing stress and make us feel calm and happy. Many doctors use games instead of medicines to help us in our wellness. Discuss and assess how games we play have changed over time and how playing helps you feel better. Communication

INDOOR GAMES

Games that we play inside a building, such as our home or our school building, are known as indoor games. Some indoor games are ludo, chess, carrom and other **board games**.

A girl and a boy playing ludo

- Name your favourite game: ____________________
- How many players are needed to play it? ____________________
- Write briefly how you play this game: ____________________

OUTDOOR GAMES

Games that we play outside are known as outdoor games. Some of the common outdoor games are cricket, badminton, kite flying, hockey, basketball, handball, volleyball, football, cycling, roller skating and many others.

Outdoor games are a good way to exercise our body and keep it healthy.

Fact Finder

Olympic Games are one of the biggest sporting events in the world. Athletes from different parts of the world participate in a variety of competitions. Find out the different games in which people compete in Olympics and discuss.

Activity Corner

Sort I as Indoor and O as Outdoor games:

1. Ludo ____________
2. Badminton ____________
3. Cricket ____________
4. Chess ____________
5. Kite flying ____________

Children love playing outdoor games in school during their lunch break or games period. Some common games they play are football, cricket, kho-kho and hide-and-seek. Which outdoor game do you like to play in school? Which game did your mother like playing when she was your age?

Myra and Harsh love playing basketball.

Our parents and grandparents used to play many games in their childhood. Many of those games were very different from the ones that we play today. Nowadays we can play on computers, mobile phones, **tablets** and other **gadgets**. However, we should also play outside in parks or gardens where we can get fresh air and exercise.

My Eco Club

Whenever we play outdoor games, we must make sure to not litter or dirty the area. When we play in parks, we should not walk on the plants or harm them. If you find trash lying on the ground, be a green hero and put it in the bin.

My India

Long before digital games and fancy toys were available, people in India played simple and creative games using easily available local things. Some Indian games can be found painted in old scriptures and even carved on temple walls. Name one game which originated in India.

GAMES IN THE PAST AND THE PRESENT

Chaupar

We played with simple toys: *pitthoo* (seven stones), *kancha* (marbles), board games like *chaupar*, kites, skipping ropes and many more!

PLAY AS WORK

Some people receive **training** in certain sports. They are paid money to play these sports just as others are paid a salary for their jobs. They are known as **professional** players or sportspeople. Some of India's famous professional players are Virat Kohli (cricket), Saina Nehwal (badminton), Neeraj Chopra (javelin throw), Manu Bhaker (Shooting) and Dipika Pallikal (squash).

Dipika Pallikal is a brilliant squash player.

Who is your favourite sportsperson? ______________

Name the sport they play: ______________________

Playing games is important. We should do our best and enjoy playing whether we win or lose. All games have rules and it is important to play according to the

Our Values

Playing games helps in building team spirit. We should not cheat or fight while playing.

- Is it alright to cheat if we are losing a game?

Let's Remember

Games We Play

- **Indoor Games** → Games we play inside a building, like ludo, chess and carom.
- **Outdoor Games** → Games we play outside, like cricket, badminton and football.
- **Games in the Past and Present** → Games in the past used to be played with simple things like stones and marbles.
- **Play as Work** → Professional players or sportspeople get money for the games they play.

New Words

Board games: Games thaat are played on a board, often using dice and other small pieces that are moved around

Gadgets: Small tools or machines that do something useful

Tablets: Small computers that are easy to carry, with a large screen

Training: The process of learning a sport or a job

Professional: Doing something as a paid job

Exercises

A. Choose the correct answers.

Remembering and Understanding

1. Which of the following can be done for recreation?
   (a) Cycling (b) Watching TV (c) Painting (d) All of these
2. Which of the following is not a board game?
   (a) Hockey (b) Carom (c) Ludo (d) Chess
3. Which of these is a game played by our grandparents and parents?
   (a) TV game (b) Game on tablet (c) Game on smartphone (d) *Kanchas*

4. Read the statements below and choose the correct option.
   Statement (A): Snakes and ladders is an indoor game.
   Statement (B): We play all games outside.
   (a) Both (A) and (B) are true, and (B) is the correct explanation of (A).
   (b) Both (A) and (B) are true, but (B) is not the correct explanation of (A).
   (c) (A) is true but (B) is false.   (d) (A) is false but (B) is true.

B. State whether true or false. Rewrite the false statements correctly.

1. We should work in our free time.
2. We can never play any games inside the house.
3. People today use fancy gadgets for playing games.
4. Our grandparents never played games in their childhood.
5. People do not play games to earn money.

C. Match the rows.

1. *Chaupar*	2. *Kanchas*	3. Playing Outdoors	4. Rules	5. Virat Kohli
(a) Fresh air	(b) Marbles	(c) Cricket	(d) Fair play	(e) Board game

D. Answer the following questions.

1. How are indoor games different from outdoor games?
2. Name any two outdoor games that were popular in olden times.
3. How are games we play today, different from those our parents played in their childhood?
4. Name any three games your grandparents must have played in their childhood.
5. Who are professional players? Name any three professional players of India and the sports they play.

Reflect and Learn

21st CENTURY SKILLS

A. Discuss: How do physical games help in building social skills? Communication

B. Think and Answer: What will happen if you have to study all day and have no time left to play or relax? Critical Thinking

C. Read the text and answer the questions: Chess is a game that started in India long ago. It is played between two people on a board with black and white squares. The game helps players think deeply and make clever moves. Playing chess is like exercise for the mind!

1. Where did chess begin? 2. What kind of game is chess—indoor or outdoor?
3. How does chess help our mind?

Project and Portfolio

A. Individual activity: Pick a sport that people play for work. Find out how many players play, the rules and what things are used. Stick pictures of players and the things needed to play on chart paper. Show and talk about it in class. C-6.2 Creativity

B. Group activity: In a group of five, design and draw a board game to play in class. Write how many players can play and the rules. Stick it on chart paper and display it. Try playing the game by following the rules. Creativity SI Arts Education

C. Interdisciplinary activity: Make a list of Indian Olympic medal winners of 2024. Add pictures, the sport and the year. Make a sports album to show in class. C-6.1 Creativity

Self-review

Colour the smileys to show how well you have understood the concepts.	Completely	Mostly	Need help
• I can recognize means of recreation and identify indoor and outdoor games.	☺	☺	☺
• I can differentiate between objects and activities of present and past (at time of the elders).	☺	☺	☺
• I can identify play and sports as work for some people.	☺	☺	☺

Teacher's Tip

Let children talk about games they play with family and friends. Discuss some games they may not know. Talk about famous players they have seen. This helps them learn how people can earn money through sports.

5 Way of Life

Learning Outcomes

The learner:
- explains the different kinds of traditional clothes worn in various parts of India.
- identifies the diversity in language and food of India.
- describes the local games commonly played.

Warm-up

Observing

Identify the different clothes that the people in these pictures are wearing and write them in the blanks given.

__________ __________ __________ C-6.2

What do you call each of the above clothes in your regional language and any other local language? Write it here.

Piece of Clothing	Name in English	Name in Your Regional Language	Name in Another Local Language
A.			
B.			
C.			

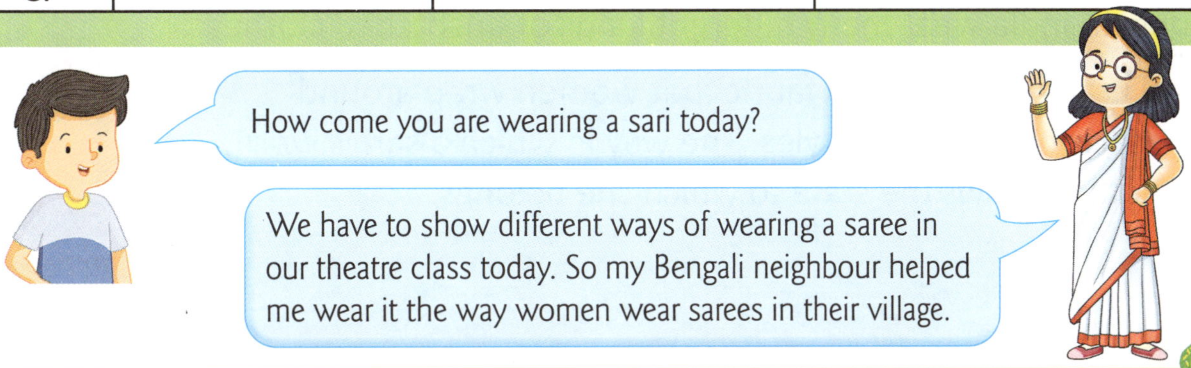

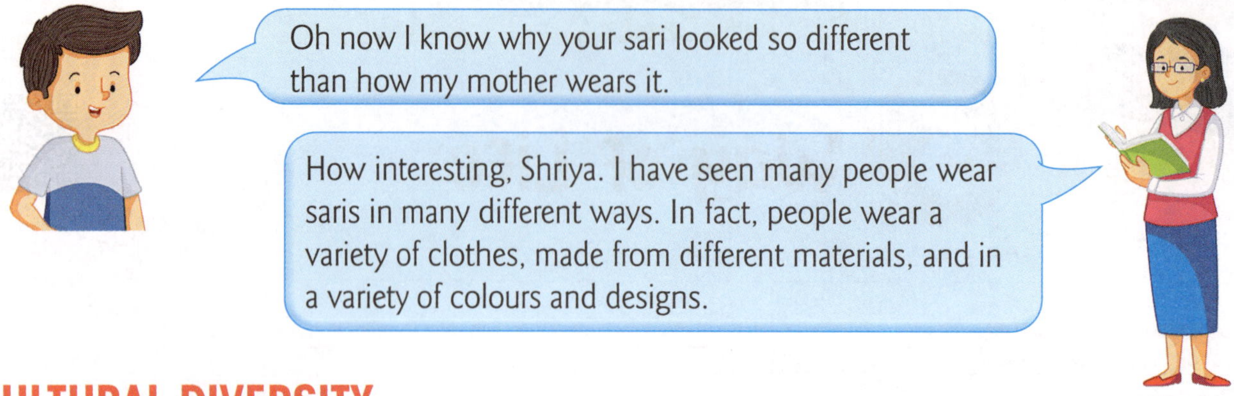

CULTURAL DIVERSITY

Every region in India has its own type of food, clothing, the way people wear clothes, as well as the languages that people speak. India is a land of **diversity**. The way we live is different in different parts of the country. We have already learnt how different festivals are celebrated in different parts of the country.

Our clothes, language, food choices, festivals, music, songs, poems and the games we play forms the culture. It differs from one region to another.

TRADITIONAL CLOTHING

The clothes people wear depends on many factors:

1. The weather and climate of the place
2. The religious beliefs of people
3. The kind of local art and craft done to decorate cloth
4. The occupations and economic welfare of people

> **Sustainable Development Goals (SDGs)**
>
> **Goal 12: Responsible Consumption and Production**
> Some clothes are made from used materials like plastic bottles or old fabric. This helps save resources and keeps our Earth clean!

In India, people wear a variety of clothes, some stitched and some unstitched.

Stitched and Unstitched Clothes We Wear

People in India wear many different kinds of unstitched clothes.

A sari is a long-unstitched fabric that women wrap around themselves in different styles. The way in which a sari is worn, sometimes shows the state to which she belongs.

A woman wearing a sari in Bengali style

For example, in Assam, women wear a *mekhla*, which is a long cloth wrapped around the waist. It is worn with a blouse and a chadar. The chadar is draped around the upper body. Blouse is a stitched garment.

> **My Eco Club**
>
> Silk is a fibre we get from silkworms. The process by which we get silk kills the worms. Therefore, we should opt for plant-based silk fibre called silk cotton. Find out what ahimsa silk is and judge whether it can be a good substitute for pure silk or not.

Women also wear a *salwar kurta* and *dupatta*. A *salwar kurta or kameez* is a **stitched** garment set, while a *dupatta* is **unstitched**. A dupatta is a long-unstitched cloth used by women to cover their heads and wrap around the upper part of their bodies. It is also known by different names such as *odhani*, *chunri* and chunni. Women in different states wear it in different ways. In Punjab, women traditionally wear it with *salwar-kameez*. In Rajasthan and Haryana, they wear it with a traditional skirt and blouse, called *lehnga-choli*. In Uttar Pradesh, they wear it with *churidaar kurta*. In Jammu and Kashmir, they wear it with *pheran*. Just like women, men also wear an unstitched cloth to cover their heads. It is called a turban or *pagri*. It is a long unstitched cloth worn on the head in different ways in different parts of the country.

A woman wearing *salwaar-kameez*

> **Activity Corner**
>
> Get a dupatta or a scarf to class and then try to tie a turban for each other in any one way. Discuss the steps where you faced a problem.

> **Fact Finder**
>
> A turban is often called a *pagri* in many parts of India. People wear the turban in many different ways and is usually tied manually. The way in which a turban is worn depicts many things about the person wearing it, their culture and beliefs.

Men also wear unstitched clothes called *lungis* and *dhotis*. Just like saris, *dhotis* and *lungis* are also tied in different ways in different states. They are usually worn with a kurta or a shirt.

DIVERSITY IN LANGUAGE AND FOOD

Though there is no national language of India, there are almost 22 officially recognised languages spoken, out of which Hindi and Urdu are most widely spoken. Every region has its own way of speaking these languages, which forms the **dialect**.

The kind of food people eat, also differs from one region to another and depends a lot on the following:

- The kind of crops grown locally: Example since mustard is extensively grown in Punjab, we usually find preparations involving mustard seeds and even leaves in their local diet.
- The climate of the place: In dry and hot places like Gujarat and Rajasthan, people eat a lot of **fermented** food and curd-based foods.
- The animals and plants naturally found in the region: Since coconut naturally and extensively grows in coastal areas, the foods involve a lot of coconut as a base in their dishes.
- The presence of locally found water bodies: Example, in coastal areas, fish becomes a staple diet due to the abundance of fish available.

Bengali mustard fish curry

LOCAL GAMES

The most common local games people play in villages include using very simple things, which are easily available.

Spinning top

People in villages still play with simpler toys. Wheel and stick game is also very popular, and so are cartwheels. Lattu or spinning top is so a very common toy people play with in villages. It is called by different names in different regions of India.

People in different regions have their own forms of music, dance and even musical instruments. They are known as folk music and dance.

My India

Each state of India has a traditional form of dance or folk dance, which is performed to celebrate many occasions and festivals, weddings or local celebrations. People wear traditional clothes for the dances and usually the dances have traditional folk musicians too. Give two reasons why people wear traditional clothes during folk dances.

Our Values

We should respect regional diversity in language, music, clothes, food, culture and even games that people play.

- In what way can you show respect for diverse cultures?
- Does this diversity appear only in India or worldwide? Discuss how food, music, language and clothing differ from one country to another. We must show respect towards all cultures.

Let's Remember

Way of Life

Cultural Diversity	India is a land of diversity and people have different food, clothing, languages and games.
Traditional Clothing	People wear different clothes in India, which are traditional and stitched or unstitched.
Diversity in Language and Food	There are many languages in India. Regions have their own unique food according to local crops and climate.
Local Games	Local games like spinning top, cartwheel, wheel and stick etc. are still played today.

New Words

Diversity: A range of many people or things that are very different from each other

Traditional clothes: Clothes worn by a particular group of people for a long time

Unstitched: Clothes that are worn without being stitched

Dialect: A form of a language that is spoken in one area of a country

Fermented: Something that causes food or drinks to become sour, bubbly, or stronger in taste.

Exercises

A. Choose the correct answers.

Remembering and Understanding

1. Which of these forms the culture of people?
   (a) Food and clothing (b) Music and dance
   (c) Festivals and languages (d) All of these
2. Which of these affects the kind of clothes people wear?
   (a) The religious beliefs (b) Local handicrafts
   (c) Weather and climate of the place (d)) All of these
3. Diversity in food depends on which of these factors?
   (a) Locally found plants and animals (b) The climate of the place
   (c)) Locally grown crops (d) All of these

4. Read the statements below and choose the correct option.
   Statement (A): There is diversity in culture in different regions.
   Statement (B): Food, language, music, art, dance, clothing and the festivals we celebrate affect the way we live.
   (a) Both (A) and (B) are true, and (B) is the correct explanation of (A).
   (b) Both (A) and (B) are true, but (B) is not the correct explanation of (A).
   (c) (A) is true but (B) is false. (d) (A) is false but (B) is true.

B. Fill in the blanks.

1. The ________________ (sari/lungi) is an unstitched garment worn by women in india
2. A ________________ (turban/lungi) is an unstitched cloth men wear over their heads.
3. There is/are ________________ (one/many) language(s) people speak in India, with regional differences.
4. The kind of food people eat is ________________ (different/same) from one region to another.
5. ________________ (Pitthoo/Lattu) refers to a top people play with in villages.

C. State whether true or false. Rewrite the false sentences correctly.

1. Everyone in India wears the same kind of clothes, depending on the weather of the place.
2. There is regional difference only in the language people speak.
3. Lungi is a common unstitched garment worn by men.
4. There is regional diversity in the food we eat.
5. Music and dance remains the same in different regions of India.

D. Answer the following questions.

1. What forms the culture of a place?
2. List three factors that affect the kind of clothes people wear in a particular region.
3. What is a sari? How is it different from a *dupatta*?
4. Explain the difference between a turban and a *lungi*.
5. What leads to regional diversity in food that people eat?

Reflect and Learn

21st CENTURY SKILLS

A. Discuss: Mention three different ways in which the sari is worn in different states.

Communication

B. Think and Answer: Why do people usually wear traditional clothes during festivals?

Critical Thinking

C. **Read the passage and answer the questions**: Kachhora is a special way tribal women in Chhattisgarh wear their saree. They wrap the saree around their body and tuck it between their legs to help them move easily while working. This style is useful for farming, cooking and dancing. The sarees are made from cotton, silk, or linen and come in bright colours and pretty patterns.

1. Who wears the Kachhora saree style?
2. Why is the Kachhora style useful for tribal women?
3. What materials are used to make them?

Project and Portfolio

21st CENTURY SKILLS

A. Individual activity: Try wearing a sari in the way it is traditionally worn in any state of India. Then talk about how different it is, to the usual way in which a saree is draped (C-1.2) Creativity

B. Group activity: In groups of five, try learning a few steps of the Bihu dance and then join together with other groups and do it (C-1.2) SI Arts Education

C. Field trip: Visit three neighbours and ask about their traditional food, clothes, and art or music of the state they belong to. Make a chart and present it in your mother tongue. (C-6.2) SI Languages

Self-review

Colour the smileys to show how well you have understood the concepts.	Completely	Mostly	Need help
• I can explain the different kinds of traditional clothes worn in various parts of India.	☺	☺	☺
• I can identify the diversity in language and food of India.	☺	☺	☺
• I can describe the local games commonly played.	☺	☺	☺

Teacher's Tip

Bring different types of saris and turbans to class so children can explore the feel and look of various fabrics. You can also give each child a dupatta and show them how it can be tied like a turban. This will help them understand traditional clothing and how it is worn in different parts of India.

Problem Solving and Life Skills

Chapter 1

1. Whom do you admire the most in your family?
2. Give two reasons why you admire them.
3. Give three ways in which you would spend time with that family member.

Chapter 2

1. How does going to a mela make you feel? Draw two pictures to show
2. Who would you like to go to mela? Give two reasons
3. How would a mela help preserve the culture of a place?

Chapter 3

1. Who is the person in the picture?
   (a) Bhagat Singh (b) Jawaharlal Nehru
   (c) Mahatma Gandhi
2. When is his birthday?
   (a) 2 October (b) 3 October (c) 4 October
3. Which festival is celebrated on his birthday?
4. Which new festival related to cleanliness is celebrated on his birthday?

Chapter 4

1.

2.

3.

1. Which of these is an outdoor game? ______________
2. Out of these games, circle the ones you have played.
3. Which of these would game labelled as 2 involve?
   (a) Eye (b Nose (c) Ear
4. Give two ways in which outdoor games have changed with digital devices.

Chapter 5

1. Which of these would be the water body where this festival would be celebrated?
   (a) Wells (b) Rivers (c) Seas and oceans
   (d) Rainwater
2. Write two ways in which such activities would help people and their lives.
3. Is it safe to use water from such a source and use it for drinking as it is? Why or why not? Give a reason.

Observing

TOGETHER IN NATURE

Plants grow tall, green and bright,
Giving us shade and fruits so right.
Animals roam, fly, swim, and play,
Each with a role in nature's way.
Humans, plants, and creatures too,
Live together—me and you!

A sheep sleeps softly under a tree,
While birds above chirp happily.
The tree gives shade, the nest a home,
Together they rest, no need to roam.
Plants, animals, and people too,
Share the Earth—me and you!

Circle Time

1. How does a tree help animals?
2. What are the different ways in which animals move?
3. Why do you think animals need to move from one place to another and plants do not?
4. How can we, plants and animals live together?
5. In what way do we share the earth with plants and animals?

6 Plants around Us

Learning Outcomes

The learner:

- observes and identifies plants growing in the immediate environment.
- classifies plants on the basis of shape, size and structure (flowers, fruits and seeds).
- explains the process of germination.
- describes what is a kitchen garden.

Warm-up

Pick some fallen leaves from any five trees around you. Look at them carefully and answer the following questions:

- Are all the leaves of the same size?
- Are all the leaves of the same shape?
- How do the leaves feel? (rough or smooth)
- Do the leaves have a smell? Name one thing that has a similar smell.
- Now paste the leaves to show a pattern.

C-1.1

I went out to a shop that sells plants with dada and was surprised to see so many different types of plants there!

Oh! So you went to a nursery? If you go to the neighbourhood park also, you will find many different types of plants growing.

Yes, I have seen a variety of plants in the park. Some are very big while some are quite small too. I have even seen some plants growing in the river too!

Is that even possible?

Yes. Many different kinds of plants grow around us. Some plants are big while some are small. Some plants grow on land and some in water. Some of them can even grow under water.

DIFFERENT KINDS OF PLANTS

Plants are of different shapes and sizes and have different kinds of leaves too.

Parts of a tree

Trees

Big, tall and strong plants are called trees. They have a thick, strong and woody stem called the trunk. Most trees have many branches. The trunk of a tree is covered by a protective layer called the bark. Trees live for many years. Some trees stay green all through the year while some **shed** most or all their leaves at least once a year.

Some of the common trees found in India are ashok, neem, peepal, gulmohar, mango, guava and coconut trees.

Activity Corner

Go to your neighbourhood park and choose any five types of trees. Place a blank white page on the barks of these trees. Take a pencil and gently rub it all over the paper. This will give you the bark print of each tree. Compare the feel, smell and patterns of barks of each of these trees.

Shrubs

Small plants with woody stems are called shrubs. Shrubs have many stems and branches and are bushy. They live for a few years. Cotton, hibiscus, tulsi (basil) and rose plants are some commonly found shrubs.

Cotton plant

Herbs

Small plants with soft green stems are known as herbs. Grass is a herb. Some commonly grown herbs are mint, spinach and coriander.

Coriander

Climbers and Creepers

Some plants have weak stems and need support, such as a wall or a stick or another tree, to grow. These plants are called climbers.

Some common examples of climbers are grapevines, money plants, morning glory and bean plants.

Bean plant

Creepers are plants with weak stems that grow along the ground. Pumpkin, watermelon, gourd and musk melon plants are common examples of creepers.

Pumpkin plant

The Sun and Plants

Plants need sunlight.

The sun is very important for plants to grow. Green plants make their own food, in the presence of sunlight. The sun is the natural source of heat and light on earth. Sun is also needed for flowers to bloom. Flowers become fruits with seeds inside them. This helps with the continuity of life. Sun is also needed to give warmth to seeds sown in soil, which helps in their germination.

GERMINATION

What happens when we sow seeds?

When seeds get the right amount of air, water and warmth, they become new plants. Seeds become new plants by the **process** of germination. The new baby plant that grows from the seed is called a seedling.

> **Sustainable Development Goals (SDGs)**
>
> **Goal 7: Affordable and Clean Energy**
> Solar energy is clean and safe for the Earth. It uses sunlight to make power without causing pollution.

LEAVES

Most plants have green leaves that grow on stems. Green leaves help the plant make its own food, and therefore leaves are also known as the kitchens of a plant.

The process of germination

A leaf has tiny holes called stomata on its underside that helps it in exchange of gases and release water after making food. The green **pigment** in a leaf is called **chlorophyll**.

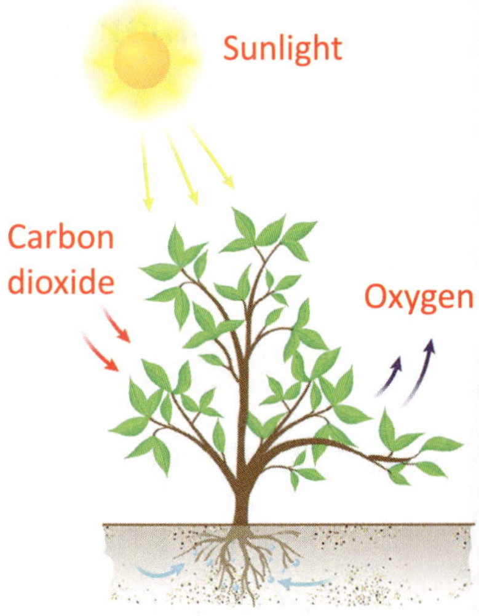

Photosynthesis

It is chlorophyll that helps green leaves to change sunlight into food by the process called photosynthesis. Photosynthesis can be defined as the process by which green plants make their own food in the presence of sunlight, water and carbon dioxide of the air.

My Eco Club

We should not pluck flowers and leaves from plants for our projects and activities. Pick the fallen ones.

My India

The Banyan tree is one of the oldest trees found in India and is often known as the 'Tree of Life'. Have you seen a banyan tree growing around you?

FLOWERS

A bee on a flower

Most plants grow flowers on their stems when they reach maturity. Flowers help plants to multiply. A flower grows from a bud. When the flower becomes a fruit, it contains seeds that can grow into new plants. Flowers of some plants like rose, jasmine, tuberose, sweet pea have a very sweet smell and are used to make perfumes too. Some flowers need help from insects like bees, ants, butterflies as well as some birds to become fruits.

Fact Finder

The Rafflesia is the world's largest flower. It has no stem or leaves. It has a very unpleasant smell. Find out the smallest flower in the world. How does the unpleasant help the Rafflesia?

TAKING CARE OF PLANTS

Plants need our love and care. When we grow plants, we need to take care of their needs too. Plants need air, water, warmth and light to grow. Since they take in nutrients from the soil they grow in, we also need to add **nutrients** to the soil from time to time. When we grow plants in water, without soil, then we have to add nutrients to the water in which they are growing.

A KITCHEN GARDEN

A kitchen garden is a small garden in your home where you grow vegetables, fruits, or herbs. It is good for the earth because it uses less water and no harmful

A kitchen garden

chemicals. You can reuse food waste to help plants grow. It gives fresh food and keeps the environment clean!

Growing small vegetables at home for our own needs can be a great way of **sustainable** living.

Be a Scientist

If you were a scientist, what kind of a plant would you study? Draw it. Write special features of the root, stem and leaf of your plant.

Our Values

We should not waste paper. Wasting paper would cause more trees to be cut down. We should try reusing as much paper as possible.

- Can you think of three ways in which you can reuse paper?

Let's Remember

Plants around Us

- Different Kinds of Plants → Plants around us are trees, shrubs, herbs, climbers and creepers.
- Germination → Seeds become new plants by germination.
- Leaves → Leaves are mostly green in colour and make food for plants.
- Flowers → Flowers helps plants multiply and become fruits.
- Taking Care of Plants → Plants need air, water, warmth and sunlight to grow.
- Kitchen Garden → A garden in your home where vegetables, fruits and herbs are grown.

New Words

Shed: Let something fall off

Process: A series of things that are done in order to achieve a particular result

Pigment: A substance that exists naturally in people, animals and plants and gives their skin, leaves, etc. a particular colour

Nutrients: A substance that is needed to keep a living thing alive and to help it to grow

Chemicals: Strong substances that can hurt people, plants, or animals if not used carefully.

Sustainable: Involving the use of natural products and energy in a way that does not harm the environment

Exercises

A. Choose the correct answers.

Remembering and Understanding

1. Which of these plants would need support to grow?
   (a) A tree because it is a big plant.
   (b) A herb because it is a small plant with soft stems.
   (c) A grapevine or a pea plant (d) A tulsi plant because it is a small plant.
2. Which of these does a plant need for germination?
   (a) Soil, air, water (b) Air, water and warmth
   (c) Air, water, soil and sunlight (d) Sunlight and air
3. Which of these are tiny holes on the underside of a leaf?
   (a) Petiole (b) Pigment (c) Stomata (d) Chlorophyll
4. Read the statements below and choose the correct option.
   Statement (A): Most leaves are green in colour.
   Statement (B): Leaves are the kitchens of plants.
   (a) Both (A) and (B) are true, and (B) is the correct explanation of (A).
   (b) Both (A) and (B) are true, but (B) is not the correct explanation of (A).
   (c) (A) is true but (B) is false. (d) (A) is false but (B) is true.

B. Fill in the blanks.

1. A tree has a thick and strong main stem called a ____________. (trunk/branch)
2. ____________ (shrubs and herbs/creepers and climbers) are plants with weak stems.
3. The presence of ____________ (chlorophyll/photosynthesis) makes a leaf green.

4. Most plants have ____________ (green/blue) leaves that grow on stems.
5. A small garden in your home where you grow vegetables, fruits and herbs is called a ____________ (Fruit/kitchen) garden.

C. Give two examples for each of the following.

1. Trees: ________________________
2. Climbers: ________________________
3. Creepers: ________________________
4. Plants with sweet smelling flowers: ________________________
5. Animals that are needed by flowers to become fruits: ________________________

D. Answer the following questions.

1. What are trees? Give two examples.
2. Explain the difference between a shrub and a herb.
3. Why do some plants need support to grow?
4. What is germination? Give the conditions needed for germination.
5. What is photosynthesis?
6. When do most plants grow flowers?

Reflect and Learn

21st CENTURY SKILLS

A. Discuss: Which is cleaner—the air in a city or the air in a forest? Why? Communication

B. Think and Answer: What do you think would happen to the air we breathe if there were no plants? Critical Thinking

C. Read the text and answer the questions: The sunflower is a tall plant with a big yellow flower that turns toward the Sun. It grows from a seed through germination and needs sunlight, water, and air to grow. Its leaves help make food using sunlight in a process called photosynthesis. Sunflowers are grown in gardens and need care like watering and sunlight every day.

1. Why must sunflowers be turning towards the sun
2. What helps the sunflower make food?
3. How will you care for a sunflower

D. Look at the picture and answer the questions: In the picture here, identify and circle in red the trees, shrub and climber plants.

Project and Portfolio

A. Individual activity: Collect a few fallen leaves and place them in a magazine to dry. Then use the dried leaves to make a Thank You card for any of your family members. C-1.1, C-1.5 Creativity SI Arts Education

B. Group activity: In groups of five, make a compost pit using an old bucket. Add soil, water, and 15 waste items like dry leaves and kitchen waste. Cover with mud and keep it outside. Water it regularly. Check after two months and note your findings. C-7.2

C. Interdisciplinary activity: Imagine yourself as a bean seed who fell on wet ground in the garden. Write your story from the seed to the plant in your own words. Draw pictures to narrate your story. C-6.2 Creativity SI Arts English

D. Field trip: Go for a walk in the school gardens or the neighbourhood park and make a list of all the different kinds of trees growing there. Get bark prints of all the different types of trees. C-4.1 Creativity

Self-review

Colour the smileys to show how well you have understood the concepts.	Completely	Mostly	Need help
• I can observe and identify plants growing in the immediate environment.	☺	☺	☺
• I can classify plants on the basis of shape, size and structure (flowers, fruits and seeds).	☺	☺	☺
• I can explain the process of germination.	☺	☺	☺
• I can describe what is a kitchen garden.	☺	☺	☺

Teacher's Tip

Take the children out for a nature walk and let them observe the different kinds of plants growing around. Let them feel the bark of a tree. Explain what a bark is and how it protects a tree. Ask each child to bring a dried, fallen leaf to class. Start the lesson by making the children feel their leaves. Ask them to observe and feel the different parts of the leaf. This will be much more useful than getting any chart or a model.

7 Animals around Us

Learning Outcomes

The learner:
- identifies simple features of animals in the immediate surroundings.
- describes need of food for animals and their homes.
- identifies insects and birds and labels their body parts.

Warm-up

Look at the picture and answer the following questions.
1. How many animals can you see in the picture?
2. Name the animals that are there in the water.
3. Name any two animals that can fly.
4. Is there any animal on the tree?
5. Why do you think a monkey has a long tail?

C-1.1

ANIMALS

We share our earth with plants and animals. Just like us even plants and animals need food, air and water to live.

Different Kinds of Animals

There are many different types of animals found on our earth. Some are big and some are small. Animals such as giraffes, cows, buffaloes, elephants, lions, tigers, hippopotamus, rhinoceroses, camels, horses, sharks, whales, dolphins and many others are big animals.

A blue whale is a big animal

The elephant is the largest land animal while the giraffe is the tallest. The blue whale is the largest animal on earth.

Most of the big animals like tigers, lions, zebras, elephants and giraffes live in forests and are known as wild animals.

A porcupine is a small animal.

Animals such as squirrels, cats, rabbits, rats, dogs, porcupines, earthworms, snails, butterflies and crabs are small animals.

Many small animals can be seen in and around our homes. We keep some small animals like cats, dogs, parrots, rabbits and small fish as pets. We should look after our pets well.

Some animals like cows, bullocks, buffaloes, hens, ducks, donkeys and sheep are domestic animals. They are tamed or **domesticated** as they are useful to us in many ways.

Fact Finder

- The cheetah is the fastest land animal.
- The largest bird in the world is the ostrich. However, it cannot fly like other birds do.

Animal Bodies

Animals have different body **structures**. Almost all animals have a head, eyes and **limbs**.

Animals like cows, horses, monkeys, goats and sheep have four legs while birds have two. Snakes and earthworms do not have legs. Some very small animals like ants, butterflies and bugs have six legs. They are called insects.

Spiders have eight legs. Tiny centipedes and millipedes have many, many legs! Birds have wings with feathers and a special mouth called a beak. Fish do not have legs. They have **fins** instead. Most animals have a tail. It can be either short or long. Animals use their tails in different ways.

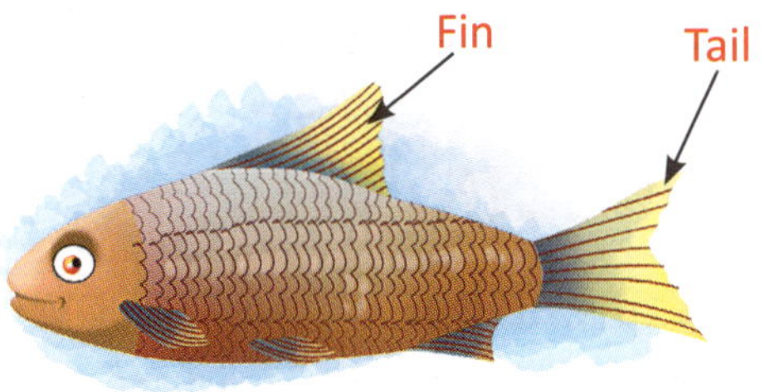

Parts of a fish

- Tails help animals to balance their bodies as they swim, hop, jump or swing from branch to branch.
- Tails help fish to change direction while swimming.
- Tails help some animals to brush away flies and other small animals from their bodies.
- Tails also help animals to show their feelings.

My Eco Club

Animals live in close contact with the nature. We should not cut down trees or pollute water because they are their home.

Animals and Their Homes

Different animals live in different homes. Sometimes they make their own homes. People also make homes to keep some animals. Some animals make very interesting homes.

Bees live in a hive.

A bird lives in a nest. An ant lives in an anthill. A mouse lives in a hole. A spider spins a web for a home. A cow lives in a shed. A horse lives in a stable. A lion lives in a den. Most animals make their homes to lay eggs and, or look after their young ones. Some animals also make homes to deal with unfavourable conditions.

Animals and Their Food

A cow is herbivorous.

Animals eat different kinds of food. Some animals eat only plants. They are called herbivorous animals. Cows, horses, giraffes and goats are some common herbivores.

Animals that hunt and eat the flesh of other animals are called carnivorous animals. Tigers, lions, cheetahs and panthers are carnivores.

Some flesh-eating animals, such as jackals and hyenas, do not hunt. They eat the leftovers of what other animals have hunted and fed upon. They also eat the flesh of animals which are already dead. They are called scavengers.

Some animals such as crows and bears eat both plants and flesh of other animals. They are called omnivores.

INSECTS

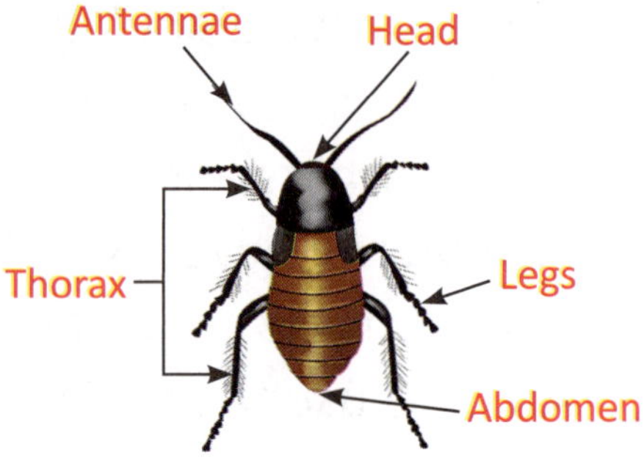

Parts of an insect

Our earth is full of creepy-crawly creatures. These include insects, worms, spiders, snails, lizards and many more. These tiny creatures are found everywhere—on land, on trees, in water and even under the ground. Different types of insects, worms, snails, spiders and reptiles can be found everywhere. They are found in gardens, in houses, on plants, in the soil and in water bodies.

An insect has six legs. Its body is divided into three parts—the head, the **thorax** and the **abdomen**. It does not have a backbone but its body has a hard covering. It has a pair of **antennae** that help it to feel and sense things.

Some insects like houseflies, cockroaches, butterflies and mosquitoes have wings that help them to fly. Some insects like grasshoppers, crickets, locusts and stick insects jump around. Some insects such as ants and termites live under the ground. Butterflies can be seen near flowers. Many insects hide themselves in the cracks and corners of the house. Some insects such as cockroaches usually come out at night.

Sustainable Development Goals (SDGs)

Goal 15: Life on Land

Earthworms make the soil fertile and help plants grow well. Make sure not to harm them. Find out how they help farmers. C-3.1

BIRDS

A bird is an animal whose body is covered with feathers. It has two wings and two legs. There are many different types of birds. Most birds can fly. A bird's body is divided into the head, the trunk and the tail. It has two pairs of limbs—the wings, towards the front, and the legs, at the back.

Parts of a bird

Different birds have different types of feet. Most of them have sharp claws at the end of their toes. Their wings are covered with feathers. These feathers are of different shapes, sizes and colours which help us to identify the bird. Some birds have very bright coloured feathers. A bird's mouth is in the form of a beak, with no teeth at all. The beak helps the bird catch food and make a nest.

Most birds are able to fly because of the following reasons.

- It has a very light body.
- It has a pair of wings covered with feathers that help it to fly.
- A bird has a **streamlined** body. This means that the shape of its body helps it to move quickly through the air.

The lines show how a bird's body cuts through the air.

Activity Corner

Use your handprint to draw a peacock! Take a blank page. Cover your left palm with blue paint. Then press your palm onto the page a few times. Draw the bird's head, eyes and beak in the centre and its feet at the bottom. C-6.2

Care of Birds and Animals

We find many birds and animals around us. There are many ways in which we could take care of the birds and animals found in our surroundings.

- We could keep clean water and food for these animals.
- We should not tease or harm them.
- We should take them to an animal hospital if there is any injured animal on the road.

My India

Salim Ali is also known as the Birdman of India. He was the first Indian to survey about birds in India and also wrote several books on them. He played an important role in setting up the Bird sanctuary in Bharatpur and worked towards preventing the destruction of the Silent Valley National Park in Kerala. How can a bird sanctuary help in saving birds? C-4.4

Our Values

We share the world with the animals. Tiny creepy crawlies are also animals that need our love and care, just like wild, domestic and pet animals. We should not harm them.

- Is it right to trap insects to play with them? Why?
- What are the different ways in which you show love and care for animals around us? C-3.1

New Words

Domesticated: Animals that are trained to obey and work for you

Structure: The way in which parts of something are connected together

Limb: An arm, a leg or a wing

Fins: The thin flat parts of a fish that help it to swim

Thorax: The middle section of an insect's body to which wings and legs are attached

Abdomen: The end part of the body of an insect that is joined to the thorax

Antennae: Two long thin parts on the heads of some insects, used to touch and feel things

Streamlined: Smooth and shaped in a way that helps something move easily and quickly, like a bird flying or a car driving fast.

Let's Remember

Animals around Us

- **Animals**
  - Animals are big, small, wild or domestic. We also keep some of them as pets. They have different body structures such as tails.
  - Different animals live in different homes. Some animals are herbivores and some are carnivores. The ones that eat both plants and flesh are omnivores.
- **Insects**
  - Insects are tiny creatures found everywhere. They have six legs and three main parts: the head, thorax and abdomen.
  - Insects fly or jump. They mostly live in the ground, corners of the house and come out at night.
- **Birds**
  - Birds are animals that fly, have a beak, wings, head, trunk, tail and legs.
  - A bird has a beak in place of teeth. It helps in catching food and making a nest.

Exercises

A. Choose the correct answers.

Remembering and Understanding

1. Which of these animals has a tail fin?
   (a) Spider needs it to make a web. (b) Snakes and earthworm need to dig.
   (c) A fish has a tail fin to change direction while swimming.
   (d) Birds need it to fly.
2. Which of these animals lives in a hole?
   (a) Cat (b) Bird (c) Mouse (d) Spider
3. Which of these body parts of an insect helps to feel and sense things around?
   (a) Thorax (b) Abdomen (c) Antennae (d) Wings
4. Read the statements below and choose the correct option.
   Statement (A): A cow is a domestic animal.
   Statement (B): Cow gives us milk.
   (a) Both (A) and (B) are true, and (B) is the correct explanation of (A).
   (b) Both (A) and (B) are true, but (B) is not the correct explanation of (A).
   (c) A is true but B is false. (d) A is false but B is true.

B. Fill in the blanks.

1. An animal that eats plants as well as the flesh of other animals is called an (herbivore/omnivore)________________
2. A spider spins a ________________ (nest/web) for a home.
3. An insect body is divided into ________________ (three/four) parts.
4. An insect has ________________ (six/eight) legs.
5. A bird has a ________________ (beak/tail) to catch its food.

C. Give two examples for each of the following.

1. Wild animals: ________________
2. Domestic animals: ________________
3. Scavengers: ________________
4. Omnivores: ________________
5. Insects that can fly: ________________

D. Answer the following questions.

1. What are wild and domestic animals? Give examples.
2. Give four reasons why most animals have a tail.
3. What are herbivorous animals? How are they different from carnivores?
4. What are scavengers? Give two examples.
5. Draw a simple diagram to show the parts of an insect's body.
6. Draw a simple diagram to show the parts of a bird body.

Reflect and Learn

21st CENTURY SKILLS

A. Discuss: Are humans herbivores, carnivores or omnivores? Give reasons.

Communication

B. Think and Answer: What are some of the ways in which one can take care of animals in our daily life?

Critical Thinking

C. Read the text and answer the questions: Lizards, garden lizards and chameleons belong to a separate family of animals called reptiles. A chameleon changes its colour according to its surroundings. This is known as camouflage.

Many reptiles such as lizards eat insects like mosquitoes, cockroaches, moths, butterflies and houseflies. They have a sticky tongue that helps them to catch insects.

1. What family of animals do lizards and chameleons belong to?
2. What special thing can a chameleon do?
3. What is the name of the trick where animals change colour to match their surroundings?
4. How do lizards catch insects?

Project and Portfolio

A. Individual activity: If you were given an opportunity to become an animal, which one would you choose to be and why? Draw an imaginary picture of yourself as an animal and write details of the food you would eat and the kind of home you would live in. C-6.2 Creativity SI Arts Education

B. Group activity: Imagine that you are a fish. Write a small paragraph about your life in a pond. C-6.2 SI English

C. Interdisciplinary activity: Imagine you are a bird and find out what kind of nest the bird makes. Draw and build that nest with your group using safe materials. Talk about what was hard and how you solved it together. C-1.5 Creativity

D. Field/Outdoor activity: Place water in a tub outside your house, in the garden or on the terrace. Keep some grains in a bowl as well. Observe and try to identify the birds that visit. Make a list. Try and draw some of them in your scrapbook.

C-4.1 SI Arts Education

Self-review

Colour the smileys to show how well you have understood the concepts.	Completely	Mostly	Need help
• I can identify simple features of animals in the immediate surroundings.	☺	☺	☺
• I can describe need of food for animals and their homes.	☺	☺	☺
• I can identify insects birds and label their body parts.	☺	☺	☺

Teacher's Tip

Let the children name a few creepy-crawly creatures they might have seen around them at home, in school, at the park, etc. Make a list on the board and then explain how they can be grouped in various categories like insects, worms, reptiles, etc. You can also take them out in the school gardens to observe and make a list of all the different animals they can see around them and group them.

8 Living in Harmony

Learning Outcomes

The learner:
- identifies ways in which plants, animals and humans depend on each other.
- lists the uses of plants.
- describes a food chain.
- explains the ways to take care of plants and animals.

Warm-up

Walk around the house and list any ten things that you eat, use or wear which come from animals. Also find out any ten things that you eat, use or wear which come from plants and draw them in a table.

	Food We Eat	Clothes We Wear	Items of Use
From Plants			
From Animals			

We live together in the world where plants, birds, animals and human beings depend on each other for many things.There is balance that exists on the earth. Let's see how we live in harmony.

BIRDS, ANIMALS AND HUMANS DEPEND ON EACH OTHER

Humans depend on animals for food, clothing, travel and transportation and even for our well-being and protection. We get milk from cows, goats and buffaloes. We get wool from sheep. Hens and ducks give us eggs. Goats, sheep and hens give us meat. Dogs guard our homes. Cows and ox help farmers by ploughing fields. Donkeys and horses carry our loads and pull carts. Some large animals such as elephants and camels can also carry loads and also help us move from one place to another.

A sheep gives us wool.

Our creepy-crawly friends are also useful to us in many ways.

- Honeybees give us honey.
- Silkworms give us silk, which is used to make clothes.
- Earthworms help to make the soil more fertile by turning and loosening it. This helps the farmers while growing crops.
- Lizards eat mosquitoes and flies, which helps us in preventing the diseases caused by them.
- We also keep some animals like dogs, cats, turtles, fish and even bunnies as pets at home. They become our companions and help us stay happy.
- Birds also give us food in the form of eggs and meat.
- Feathers of birds are used as fillings for jackets, coats, quilts and even mattresses.
- Droppings of some birds are used as manure to make the soil fertile.

A silkworm gives silk for saris.

Animals and birds depend on humans for love and care, so that their numbers do not reduce. Some animals also depend on humans to provide them with food and shelter.

My Eco Club

We must prevent clearing of forests, and pollution. These lead to the loss of home for the birds, harming them and reducing their numbers. When we build tall buildings, it harms the flight of birds

Activity Corner

Collect fallen leaves from the garden and paste them to make any one insect that is useful to us. Make sure you pick up fallen twigs to make the legs of the insect. Discuss how many different kinds of leaves you used, and how this insect is useful to us.

PLANTS ARE USEFUL TO US

Just like animals, even plants are useful to us in many ways and are our friends. Plants are very important for both humans and animals. They give us food like fruits, vegetables and grains. Animals eat plants like grass and leaves to live.

Plants also help us by cleaning the air and giving us oxygen. We use plants to make clothes, medicines, and even houses. Without plants, life would be very hard!

Uses of plants

We should not burn leaves that have fallen off. People usually collect these leaves and leave them to rot in a pit mixed with some soil and water. After a few months, they turn into manure or compost which can be used to make the soil of their fields and gardens fertile, and hence help the plants. A pit which is used for composting is called a **compost pit**.

Fact Finder

The tea we drink comes from the leaves of the tea plant. These leaves are plucked, dried and packed before we buy them from shops. Find out how tea came to India, from China, its country of origin. Discuss in class.

PLANTS AND ANIMALS DEPEND ON EACH OTHER

Butterflies help in pollination.

Trees give shelter to many animals such as birds, monkeys and squirrels. Birds make nests on tree branches. Plants on the other hand depend on animals for pollination and seed formation. They also depend on animals to take their seeds far from the mother plant to ensure their growth. We call this **dispersal** of seeds. Some animals like earthworms, slugs and snails help the soil to aid plant growth. Body wastes of some animals help to provide nutrients to the soil, which the plants use by absorbing it through their roots. Green plants also provide food for animals. There is a whole food chain that exists in nature.

My India

Sal trees are important to adivasi or tribal people. They believe a goddess called Sarna Maa lives in these trees and keeps their village safe. They celebrate the Sarhul festival, the name meaning 'worship of the Sal tree'. How does the belief of a plant being sacred helps it?

THE FOOD CHAIN

Let's look at how balance of energy is maintained in nature.

- The sun is the primary source of **energy**. Green plants convert sunlight to make their own food using air, and water through the process of photosynthesis. Hence green plants are also known as primary **producers** of food.
- Animals depend directly or indirectly on plants for their food and show different food habits. They are known as **consumers**.
- Herbivorous animals like cow, buffalo, horse, goat sheep etc as well as omnivores like crow and bear eat grasses and other plants.
- Carnivores like lion, tiger, and leopard etc and omnivores eat the herbivores.
- When these animals die, their body is eaten by scavengers and then after their bodies rot, the nutrients come back into the soil.

This chain like reaction continues in nature and energy continues to flow from one level to another. In a food chain, energy flows from one level to another. Green plants make their own food by using the sun's energy and converting it into food. A herbivore eats the plant. Then, a carnivore eats the herbivore. This is like a chain that the plants and animals form in nature.

This chain of eating habits that show how plants are eaten by animals, and then animals are eaten by other animals is called a **food chain**.

The food chain

SENSITIVITY TOWARDS PLANTS, BIRDS AND ANIMALS

Many plants, birds and animals depend on the environment for their survival. It is important to keep our air, and water clean and protect our forests. Several human activities have caused a lot of harm to the environment over time. This has led to loss of plants, animals and birds.

We need to protect our forests, water bodies and even improve the air quality to protect animals from disappearing from the Earth.

- Forests and water bodies are home to a large variety of animals. We should prevent cutting down of trees and keep our water bodies clean.

- Measures are now being taken by governments all across the world to save forests. Care is being taken to make strict laws against felling of trees, pollution of water bodies and even air pollution.

We need to be sensitive towards the needs of other living beings that we share the Earth with.

Sustainable Development Goals (SDGs)

Goal 15: Life on Land

Wildlife sanctuaries help in conserving forests and help in protecting animals and birds that live there. However, greed can make people use illegal means to kill animals in the wild for their valuable body parts like tusks, horns, fur, skin etc. We need to be mindful of our choices and help to save other living beings on earth.

Our Values

Our choices affect nature. We should use eco-friendly products and be kind to plants and animals. Let us care for the Earth and not harm it by being selfish.

- Do you think we can help preserve our forests by making wise choices in our day-to-day life? How?

Let's Remember

Living in Harmony

Birds, Animals and Humans Depend on Each Other	Humans depend on animals and plants. Animals and birds depend on humans for love and care.
Plants Are Useful to Us	Plants give us oxygen, shade, food, clothes and medicine. They give food and shelter to animals.
Plants and Animals Depend on Each Other	Trees give sheltet to many animals. Animals help plants by pollination and dispersal of seeds.
The Food Chain	The chain of eating habits that show how plants are eaten by animals, and then animals are eaten by other animals is called a food chain.
Sensitivity towards Plants, Birds and Animals	We need to be sensitive towards the needs of other living beings that we share the earth with.

New Words

Compost pit: A pit in where organic wastes can be dumped to rot and make manure

Dispersal: The process by which seeds are taken away from the mother plant

Producers: Green plants that start the food making process on earth

Consumers: Animals that consume what producers make

Energy: The strength, effort and enthusiasm required for physical or mental activity, work, etc.

Food chain: A chain that links plants and animals with their eating habits to show how energy flows in nature

Exercises

A. Choose the correct answers.

Remembering and Understanding

1. What do we get from honeybees?
   (a) Silk (b) Honey (c) Milk (d) Wool
2. Which animal helps farmers by ploughing fields?
   (a) Dog (b) Horse (c) Ox (d) Cat
3. What is a compost pit used for?
   (a) To grow flowers (b) To store water
   (c) To make manure (d) To keep animals
4. What do green plants give us?
   (a) Oxygen (b) Meat (c) Wool (d) Eggs
5. Read the statements below and choose the correct option.
   Statement (A): Earthworms are friends of farmers.
   Statement (B): Earthworms help make the soil fertile.
   (a) Both (A) and (B) are true, and (B) is the correct explanation of (A).
   (b) Both (A) and (B) are true, but (B) is not the correct explanation of (A).
   (c) (A) is true but (B) is false.
   (d) (A) is false but (B) is true.

B. Fill in the blanks.

1. Hens give us ________________.
2. Earthworms loosen the ________________ and thus help farmers.

3. The ____________________ is the primary source of energy.
4. Green plants make their own food by the process of ____________________.
5. In a food chain, green plants are ____________________.

C. State whether true or false. Rewrite the false statements correctly.

1. Only plants give us food to live.
2. Animals help to disperse seeds.
3. Plants and animals depend on each other in many ways.
4. Green plants are primary producers of food on earth.
5. We need to be sensitive towards the needs of other living beings.

D. Answer the following questions.

1. Give three things that we get from animals for food.
2. How do animals and plants help us in our clothing?
3. How do birds help us in our daily life?
4. Write five key things we get from plants, besides food.
5. What is a food chain? Explain with an example.
6. Write three ways in which we can help plants and animals.

Reflect and Learn

21st CENTURY SKILLS

A. Discuss: Why is composting better than burning leaves? Communication

B. Think and Answer: Do you think we should be thankful to animals and birds around us? Give five reasons. Critical Thinking

C. Read the passage and answer the following questions: Meera was helping in her school garden. She saw butterflies sitting on flowers and birds eating insects. She learned that plants give food to insects, insects are eaten by birds, and birds help keep the garden clean. This is called a food chain. Plants and animals all help each other and are important for nature.

1. What did Meera see in the garden?
2. What is a food chain?
3. How do birds help in the garden?

Project and Portfolio

A. Individual activity: Place water in a tub outside your house, in the garden or on the terrace. Keep some grains in a bowl as well. Observe and try to identify the birds that visit. Make a list. Try and draw some of them in your scrapbook.

C-6.2 Creativity

B. Interdisciplinary activity: Use clip arts in computer, or search the internet for pictures of animals and then create a picture of any food chain that exists on a tree. Take a printout and then talk about it in class, explaining how energy flows in that food chain.

C-1.3 SI Computer Science

C. Field Trip: Go to a park or a garden and look for bird feathers. Try to guess which bird the feathers would belong to. Then write different ways you would use those feathers and make a feather album, appreciating all that the birds do for us.

C-6.1 Creativity

Self-review

Colour the smileys to show how well you have understood the concepts.	Completely	Mostly	Need help
• I can identify ways in which plants, animals and humans depend on each other.	☺	☺	☺
• I can list the uses of plants.	☺	☺	☺
• I can describe a food chain.	☺	☺	☺
• I can explain the ways to take care of plants and animals..	☺	☺	☺

Teacher's Tip

Ask children to name animals and plants they have seen around them. Encourage them to connect how they are dependent on each other.

Problem Solving and Life Skills

Chapter 6

Observe the picture given here and then answer the questions.

1. Which of these parts of a plant are stored in the jar here?
   (a) Fruit (b) Stem (c) Leaf (d) Seed
2. Which of these is the main reason why new plants are not growing inside the jar?
   (a) There is less warmth. (b) There is no water.
   (c) There is no soil. (d) All of these

Chapter 7

1. Recall any five animals that you can find in your immediate surroundings. Draw and name them to complete the table below:

Name of the animal	Drawing of the animal	Number of legs it has	Can it fly?	Place where you saw it

2. What would happen to each of them if there were no plants in the surroundings? Think and write any three problems these animals would face.
   (a) ______________________________
   (b) ______________________________
   (c) ______________________________

Chapter 8

1. 

2. 

3. 

4. 

1. What do these pictures depict?
   (a) Food habits (b) Food chain (c) Food grains
2. Which of these is the natural source of all energy?
   (a) Sun (b) Green plants (c) Animals
3. Which of these animals would you replace animal number 3 with?
   (a) Cow (b) Fox (c) Tiger

Observing

PRECIOUS WATER

Water, water, everywhere!
Can we afford even a drop to spare?
Several litres a day you spill,
Bathing under a shower, but no bucket to fill.
When you brush your teeth and tongue
Do you let the water run?
That will also go down the drain,
And then keep waiting for the rain.
I see how my mother cooks,
Water is not wasted, she always looks.
Always fixes the leaking taps and pipes,
Can we risk ours and other's lives?
Can we afford even a drop to spare?
When water is not everywhere!

Circle Time

1. What are the different ways in which we use water in our daily life?
2. What are the different ways in which water is getting wasted in the poem?
3. Why is it important to save water?
4. How can we save water while bathing?
5. Imagine what our life would be like if there was no water in our taps for one day? Discuss.

9 Water for Life

Learning Outcomes

The learner:
- explains uses of water in daily life.
- identifies the sources of water and ways in which it can be stored.
- describes ways to save water.

Warm-up

- Make a list of all the different ways in which you use water at home.
- Then, circle all those that leads to wastage of water in some way.
- Write all that you can do to prevent wastage of water at home.

C-4.3

I got a dream that I opened the tap and there was no water. It was so scary !

Our lives would be so difficult if there was no water !

Yes, water is very important for life on earth. There would be no life on earth if there no water. Plants, animals and even us need water to live. There are many uses of water. Let us start looking them.

My Eco Club

We should not waste water. By making wise choices, we can save water. C-4.4

USES OF WATER

We use water for many purposes.

- We need water for drinking, cooking, washing, bathing and cleaning.
- Farmers need water to grow crops.

- Some factories need water to make things we use.
- Water is used to produce electricity.
- Water is also used for many sports like surfing, rafting, swimming, etc.
- In India, rivers and other water bodies are an important part of religious festivals such as the Chhath Puja in Bihar and the boat races held during the Onam festival in Kerala.
- Water bodies such as rivers, seas and oceans are also used by boats or ships to move from place to place. Let us learn more about our water bodies.

Chhath puja

Fact Finder

The rain gauge is an instrument used to measure the amount of rainfall that a place receives. Find out how a rain gauge works.

WATER BODIES AROUND US

There are many sources of water found on earth. We also get water from rain, called rainwater. Rainwater fills ponds, lakes and rivers and is also the purest form of water.

Water is present in many bodies that are called water bodies. We must keep our water bodies clean.

STORAGE OF WATER

Water can be stored in many ways to be used later. In villages, people usually store water in earthenware pots—called *ghadas* and *surahis*—or in covered buckets. Dams, tube wells, wells and canals are man-made structures for storing water.

My India

People in ancient India were smart **engineers**. They built stepwells called *baolis* to collect rainwater. Stepwells have big steps that go down deep into the ground. When it rained, water filled the stepwell, and people had water even in summers. The villagers used the water thus stored for drinking, cooking, and helping their animals. Stepwells have been very useful to save and store water especially in dry states of Rajasthan and Gujarat. Why did people build stepwells?

In cities, water is stored in tanks. There is a proper system of water storage and distribution managed by the water works department that distributes water in different neighbourhoods through pipelines.

A clay *ghada*

People have underground tanks as well as overhead ones. These tanks are filled up from the main water supply through pipelines. When we open taps, we get water from these tanks, through connected pipes.

A water reservoir

Tanks should be kept clean and covered so that germs do not breed in them.

People also collect rainwater in containers and in specially made **reservoirs**. This process is known as rainwater harvesting. Rainwater is collected so that it can be used later, when there is no rain

AVAILABILITY OF WATER RESOURCES

Our earth is known as the Blue Planet because almost three out of four parts of the earth's surface is covered with water. However, water is considered scarce on earth because most of the water is found in the seas and oceans. However, sea water is too salty to drink. Fresh water is present in lakes, rivers and under the ground. Water is also present in the form of snow on high mountains and in the form of water vapour in the air. There are different natural sources of water like rivers, ponds, lakes, and rain. Rain is the most important source of water. It is the purest form of natural water. River water is another main source of fresh water.

Activity Corner

Observe and draw any five types of containers in which water is stored in your home.

- Are these containers broad or narrow?
- What are they made of?
- Number them from 1 to 5, according to their storage capacity.
  1= least 5 = maximum

Water found under the ground is known as groundwater. Rainwater seeps down from the top layer of the soil and rocks and collects as groundwater. The level at which groundwater is found under the ground is called the water table.

The cyclical process by which water is circulated on earth, by changing its form from water to **water vapour** and then back to water again is called the water cycle.

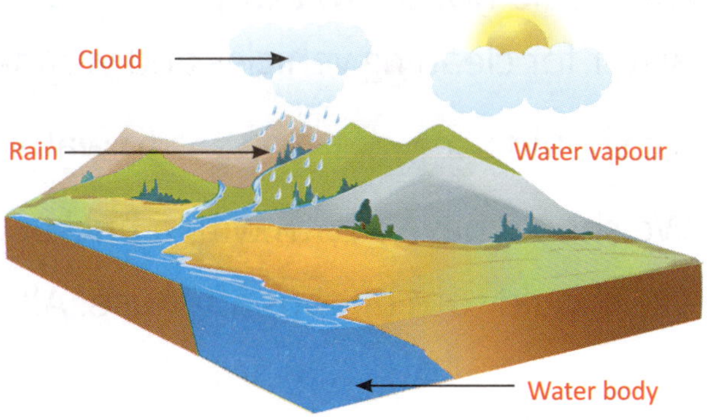

Water cycle

We can get underground water by digging wells. Tube wells are used by farmers to get groundwater for **irrigation**. This water is pumped to the surface by using an electric motor. Sometimes, hand pumps are used to draw water from the ground.

We need freshwater water to live, for drinking, cooking, washing, cleaning, growing crops, etc. Most of the freshwater is locked up as snow or present as ground water. Thus, fresh water is **scarce** and should not be wasted.

How to Save Water?

It is important to use water wisely and not waste it. We know that river water and groundwater are the two main sources of water. Most of the rivers in our country are fed by rain. This means that these rivers dry up when there is less or no rain. Since we keep using groundwater, the water table needs to be charged regularly. Rain helps in recharging the water table. If there is no rain, the groundwater will also become scarce. Some of the common reasons for shortage of water are:

- The **population** is increasing very fast. Thus, more water is being used than what is available.
- Forests help causing rainfall but they are being cut down rapidly.
- Water bodies are not getting recharged as fast as they are getting used up.
- A lot of water is getting wasted every day.

We need to use water wisely, or else the day is not too far when water will get really scarce. Here are some ways in which we can save water.

- We should not keep water running from open taps for brushing, shaving or washing clothes. We should fill water in buckets and use mugs instead.

A bucket and mug

- We should not throw away soapy water while washing clothes. We can use that water for cleaning vehicles and verandahs.
- We should use watering cans to water plants instead of using a hosepipe.
- We should have a bath with a bucket and a mug instead of a shower.
- We should turn off taps after use. All leaking pipes and taps should be repaired.

A leaking tap

- We should adopt methods of rainwater harvesting at home in schools and in our neighbourhoods.
- We should plant more trees to **conserve** water.
- We should not pollute water bodies. Wastes from our homes and factories should not be dumped in the water bodies as that makes water unfit for use.

Drinking Water

All places do not get enough water to meet the needs of everyone. In some places, people need to travel long distances to fetch water from a well or a pump. In many villages, sometimes, people have to stand in queue for hours at a well or a tap to get a bucket of water for their families. In some of the poorer and more crowded areas in cities, also called slums, people often have to wait in a queue for long to fetch water. Sometimes water tankers are used to supply water to these places.

People standing in a line for water in a slum

Sustainable Development Goals (SDGs)

Goal 10: Reduced Inequalities

Earlier, in villages, wells and tanks were owned by a few rich people. Poor people could not take water from these sources. However, today, every person has the right to use clean water from a common water source. In both villages and cities, it is the duty of the local government to provide safe drinking water to all people. Do you think it is alright to deny people the right to drinking water? Why or why not? What would you do if someone in your school was not allowed to drink water from the same tap as others? Would you find it just or unfair? Discuss.

Clean Water

A water purifier

Water that is fit for drinking is called potable water. We should not drink water directly from a tap or a well as it can carry many tiny germs that cause diseases. There are many ways in which we can make water fit for drinking. Water can be boiled before drinking. This kills **germs** present in water. Water can also be filtered to remove dust and mud from it. However, simple filtering does not kill germs.

Nowadays, special filters are available that remove several kinds of germs easily. We should drink only clean water. Drinking water should be stored in clean vessels that are kept covered.

Our Values

The water present on the earth is meant for all living beings. Thus, we should save every drop of water.

- Would it help if everyone saved a little bit of water every day? How?

Let's Remember

Water for Life

- **Uses of Water** → We need water for cooking, bathing, drinking, growing crops, electricity and festivals.
- **Water Bodies around Us** → Rainwater, ponds, rivers and lakes are some natural sources of water.
- **Storage of Water** → Water is stored in earthen pots, buckets, tanks, dams, tube wells, canals and wells.
- **Availability of Water Resources**
  - → Rainwater and rivers are the two main sources of water. Fresh water is important for living.
  - → Fresh water is scarce so we should save water by taking steps to ensure it is not wasted or polluted.
  - → Not everyone gets drinking water. Water fit for drinking is potable water. Boiling water kills germs.

New Words

Engineers: People who design and build something

Reservoir: A lake or tank where water is stored for later use

Water vapour: The form that water takes when heated

Irrigation: Man-made ways of supplying water to farms

Scarce: Only available in small quantities

Population: The number of people who live in a place

Conserve: To protect something and prevent it from being changed or destroyed

Germs: A very small living thing that can cause infection and disease

Exercises

A. Choose the correct answers.

Remembering and Understanding

1. Which of these is a natural source of water?
   (a) Lakes (b) Rain (c) Rivers (d) All of these
2. Which of these are man-made sources of water?
   (a) Canals (b) Wells (c) Tube wells (d) All of these
3. Which of these helps farmers to get groundwater for irrigation?
   (a) Ponds (b) Tube wells (c) Pipelines (d) Ghada
4. Which of these can be used to store water at home?
   (a) Overhead tanks (b) Earthenware pots (c) Buckets (d) All of these
5. Read the statements below and choose the correct option.
   Statement (A): Drinking water is called potable water.
   Statement (B): Water should be cleaned before drinking.
   (a) Both (A) and (B) are true, and (B) is the correct explanation of (A).
   (b) Both (A) and (B) are true, but (B) is not the correct explanation of (A).
   (c) A is true but B is false. (d) A is false but B is true.

B. Fill in the blanks.

1. Farmers need water to grow ____________. (crops/ religious things)
2. In villages, people usually store water in ______________ (earthenware/ glass) pots or buckets.
3. Almost three out of four parts of the Earth's surface is covered with water, it is still considered ______________ (scarce/abundant) on earth.

4. Most of the fresh water is locked up as ____________ (snow/ salty water) on the mountains or present as ____________ (lakes/ ground water).
5. Water that is fit for drinking is called __________ (ground/ potable) water.
6. ____________ (Boiling/ Simple filtering) kills germs in water.

C. State whether true or false. Rewrite the false statements correctly.

1. We need water only for drinking.
2. People store water only in underground tanks.
3. The water table needs to be recharged regularly.
4. Using a hosepipe to water plants saves water.
5. We should drink water directly from a tap or a well.
6. Boiling kills the germs present in water.

D. Answer the following questions.

1. List any five natural sources of water.
2. Write any five uses of water.
3. Why is usable water so scarce on the earth?
4. Write a short note on storage of water.
5. What is rainwater harvesting? How is it useful?
6. Give five ways in which we can use water wisely.

Reflect and Learn

21st CENTURY SKILLS

A. Discuss: Can rainwater harvesting help people who live in dry places such as deserts? How? Communication

B. Think and Answer: When there are so many water bodies on the Earth, then why do we find it scarce? Critical Thinking

C. **Read the text and answer the questions:** Crops differ in their water needs. Some crops like rice need a lot of standing water to grow. Find out how much water is needed to grow wheat, millets and other crops. A lot of water goes into growing food.

1. Do you think we should waste food?
2. By wasting food, we also waste water. Do you agree?

D. Look at the picture and answer the questions:

1. What is shown here?
2. What is it made of?
3. What is it used for?
4. Name one other object used for the same purpose.

Project and Portfolio

A. Individual activity: Present a report in class on how drinking water is cleaned and stored at home. C-6.2 SI English

B. Group activity: In groups of five, interview any three families on the following:

- Containers that they use for storing water and how often they are cleaned
- The materials that these containers are made of
- Whether they use running water or mugs for brushing their teeth
- Whether they have a bath with a shower or a bucket C-6.1 Collaboration

Collect the information and make a report out of it. Present your report in class.

C. Interdisciplinary activity: In groups of five prepare a one act play to spread the message to keep water bodies clean. Together, write the script, and then act it out. C-4.4 Creativity Collaboration SI Arts Education

D. Field Visit: Organise a visit to a local water treatment plant and see how water is purified there and sent to our homes. Make a list of five questions to ask people at the plant before going to collect information. Discuss your findings. C-2.1 Collaboration

Self-review

Colour the smileys to show how well you have understood the concepts.	Completely	Mostly	Need help
• I can explain uses of water in daily life.	☺	☺	☺
• I can identify the sources of water and ways in which it can be stored.	☺	☺	☺
• I can describe ways to save water.	☺	☺	☺

Teacher's Tip

Let the children talk about the various ways in which they have seen people wasting water. Discuss why water is scarce despite the fact that so much of the surface of the earth is covered with water. Perhaps children could be asked to make rough guess of how much water is being wasted in litres.

10 Our Food

Learning Outcomes

The learner:

- describes the importance of food for good health.
- explains the sources of food.
- identifies the meals of the day and food requirements of different family members.
- identifies healthy food and differentiates between fresh and rotten food.
- lists the various regional dishes of India.

Warm-up

Draw three foods that each of your family members likes to eat the most. C-2.3

You	Your Sibling (s)	Your Father	Your Mother	Your Grandparents

Assess which is the most preferred food of the family: ____________________

We eat a variety of food at home. I wonder why?

In my family, everyone eats different kinds of food. This confuses me.

We eat different types of food, to meet the different nutrition needs of our body. The nutrition that we need also differs with age. Let us first understand why we need food.

IMPORTANCE OF FOOD

Food is important to us for many reasons. It gives us energy, helps us grow and also protects us from diseases. There are three different kinds of food.

Energy-giving Foods

They contain carbohydrates that give energy to our body. For example, wheat, rice, sugar, etc.

Body-building Foods

They contain proteins which help the body to grow and repair the injured parts. For example, eggs, milk, meat.

Protective Foods

Certain foods like fruits, vegetables, milk and nuts give us the minerals and vitamins that help us to stay healthy and protect us from diseases.

We must eat all these different types of food in the right amounts and drink plenty of water to stay healthy and strong. A diet that contains all the nutrients which help us to grow, work and stay healthy is called a balanced diet.

A balanced diet

Sustainable Development Goals (SDGs)

Goal 2: Zero Hunger

The Akshaya Patra Foundation is a group that helps end hunger by giving free, healthy meals to school children. Their food helps children stay strong, learn better, and go to school every day. Discuss how you can help children who are unable to bring food to school.

SOURCES OF FOOD

All the different kinds of food that people eat come from either plants or animals.

My Eco Club

Eating food that is locally grown helps conserve energy and resources, thus helping environment.

Food from Plants

Plants give us a wide variety of food products.

- We get fruits, vegetables, **cereals**, pulses and nuts from plants.
- Plants also give us spices and herbs to add flavour to our food.
- We eat fruits of many plants. Sometimes we eat different parts of a plant as vegetables.

Fruits and vegetables

Different types of pulses

Different types of spices

Parts of a plant eaten	Name of the vegetable
Root	Carrot, radish, turnip
Stems	Potato, ginger
Leaves	Spinach, mint, coriander and lettuce
Flowers	Cauliflower and broccoli
Fruits	Ladyfinger, tomato and brinjal
Seeds	Peas and beans as pulses
Grains	Rice wheat, maize, jowar and bajra as cereals

- We also get sugar, tea and coffee from plants.

Food from Animals

Animals like cows, buffaloes and goats give us milk. People in deserts get milk from camels, while people living on high mountains get milk from sheep and yaks. Milk is also used to make other products like curd, cheese, paneer, ghee and butter. These are known as milk products or **dairy** products.

Dairy products

Seafood

Animals also give us meat and eggs. We get eggs mainly from hens, ducks and geese. We also eat fish of different kinds such as rohu, pomfret, sardine, mackerel, salmon and trout. Besides fish, people also eat other seafood like prawns, crabs, lobsters and oysters.

People who eat only food from plants are called vegetarians. People who also eat meat, fish and eggs are called nonvegetarians.

Are you a vegetarian or a non-vegetarian?

____

Fact Finder

There are people who do not eat any foods from animal sources. They are called **vegans**. Vegans do not even eat dairy and dairy products.

Meals and Eating in the Family

We mostly eat three meals a day—breakfast in the morning, lunch at noon and dinner in the evening. It is important to eat our meals on time.

In most families, all the family members eat the same kind of food most of the time. But sometimes, elders like to eat simple food and children prefer to eat junk food.

Activity Corner

Do you have fixed meal times at home? ____________

Does everyone in your home eat together? ____________

Draw the big and small hands of the clock to show what time you have the following meals: Breakfast, lunch, dinner.

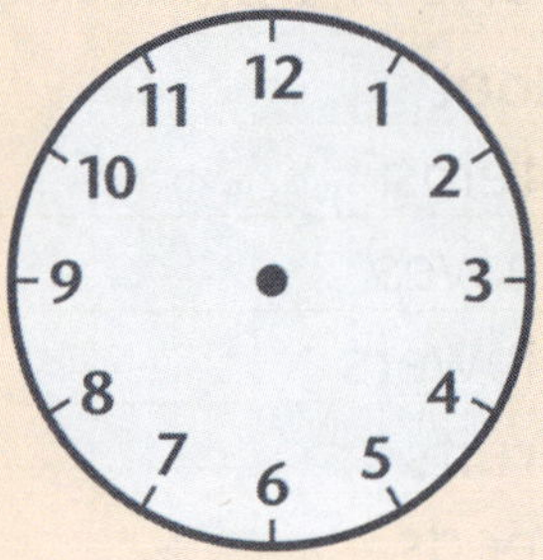

Babies drink milk as they do not have teeth. After four months of age, they start eating soft foods like mashed potato, porridge, khichdi, mashed banana, steamed apple and cereals. When they are about a year old, they are slowly introduced to solid food. The amount of food we eat depends on our age and the kind of physical work we do. Growing children and people who do more physical work need more food to eat.

Old people generally prefer to eat less. They also prefer to eat soft food as it is easier to chew and digest.

HEATHY FOOD

It is very important to wash fruits and vegetables well before eating or cooking them. Washing them with clean water removes all the germs. Similarly, some foods like potatoes, lady finger and even brinjal should be cooked well before eating. Eating them raw can be unhealthy. However, we can eat some vegetables like carrots, cabbage and cucumbers raw. Sometimes, when the food gets stale, or spoilt then it gets a growth on it, and becomes smelly. This spoils the food and should not be eaten. Though food stays for a long time in the fridge without getting spoilt, it does rot after some time. Eating spoilt food can make us sick.

Washing vegetables

Food should be washed and well-cooked before eating. Cooking destroys germs in food. However, cooking food for too long may destroy some important nutrients present in the food.

Food that is eaten raw should be washed well and should not be stored for too long. Fresh food that is cooked at home is good for health as it has **nutrients** that we need.

Junk food

Some foods like chips, burgers and ice creams are tasty but they do not give us nutrition. These are known as junk foods. Eating junk food all the time can be very harmful to our health.

Fresh Food and Rotten Food

Foods can get spoiled if not stored the right way. We know they are spoilt when they develop

- An unpleasant odour
- A bad taste and
- A bad texture

My India

In Rajasthan, people use thick mud walls, underground storage and clay pots to keep food cool naturally. These traditional methods help prevent spoilage even in the desert heat. How would mud keep the walls cool?

When foods get spoilt, they start looking **slimy** and sometimes even get a growth on top. Eating spoilt food can make us ill. We should not eat spoilt food and remove it if it gets any growth or discolouration. We can prevent food from spoilage for some time by drying them or putting them in the fridge.

REGIONAL FOOD

People eat a variety of foods depending on the place they live in, the food habits of the family and foodstuffs that are readily available.

Idli, sambhar and vada

Example, in most parts of South India, people enjoy idli, sambhar, vada, dosa, and coconut chutney. Delhi, with some of the best street foods in the country is also considered the street food capital of India. In the West, people often eat dhokla, thepla, and pav bhaji. Eastern states are known for fish curry, *pakhala bhata* (curry rice), and *rosogolla*. In the Northeast, momos, bamboo shoot dishes, and *eromba* are popular. Each region has its own distinct flavours and specialties.

Our Values

We should always try to finish our food and not waste it. There are many people in the world who do not get enough to eat.

- If you are given some food that you do not enjoy eating but you know that it is good for your health, what would you do?

Let's Remember

Our Food

- **Importance of Food** → Food gives us energy, helps us grow and protects us from diseases.
- **Sources of Food** → We get food from plants and animals. We get fish and seafood from the sea.
  → We eat three meals in a day: Breakfast, lunch and dinner
- **Healthy Food** → Eating nicely washed fruits and vegetables is good for our health. We should not eat stale food.
- **Regional Food** → People eat a variety of foods depending on the place they live in, the food habits of the family and foodstuffs that are readily available.

New Words

Cereals: Food made from the grain of cereals, often eaten for breakfast with milk

Dairy: Milk, cheese and other milk products

Nutrients: Substances that we need to grow healthy and strong

Slimy: Any unpleasant thick liquid substance

Exercises

A. Choose the correct answers.

Remembering and Understanding

1. Which of these is safe to eat?
   (a) Raw food that is well washed. (b) Food that is cooked well.
   (c) Food that is not slimy or has a bad odour. (d) All of these.
2. Which of these is true about junk foods?
   (a) They are very nutritious and tasty. (b) They are harmful to our health.
   (c) Their cooking destroys important nutrients.
   (d) They are healthy and are eaten raw.
3. Which of these indicates that the food has got spoilt?
   (a) It has a slimy look. (b) It gives off a foul odour.
   (c) There is a growth on it. (d) All of these
4. Read the statements below and choose the correct option.
   Statement (A): We can group foods into three main food groups.
   Statement (B): Different foods give us different nutrients.
   (a) Both (A) and (B) are true, and (B) is the correct explanation of (A).
   (b) Both (A) and (B) are true, but (B) is not the correct explanation of (A).

(c) A is true but B is false. (d) A is false but B is true.

B. Fill in the blanks.

1. Peas and beans are called ________________ (cereals/pulses) and are actually seeds of plants.
2. People who eat meat are also called ________________. (vegetarians/non-vegetarians)
3. All fruits and vegetables should be eaten ________________. (cooked/well washed)
4. We ________________ (should/should not) eat food that has a slimy feel.
5. ________ (Fish/Chicken) curry is a very popular dish in the eastern states of India.

C. Give three examples for each of the following.

1. Body building foods: ________________________________
2. Stems we eat: ________________________________
3. Foods from plants: ________________________________
4. Dairy products: ________________________________
5. Foods that can be eaten raw: ________________________________
6. Junk Foods: ________________________________

D. Answer the following questions.

1. What are the main types of foods? Give two examples of each.
2. What is a balanced diet?
3. Differentiate between vegetarian and non-vegetarian food habits.
4. How can we make out if a food is fit for eating or not?
5. What are junk foods? Give three examples.

Reflect and Learn

21st CENTURY SKILLS

A. Discuss: Why should we keep our food covered? Communication

B. Think and Answer: Name any three foods that the following people should eat, according to what they do. 1. A Class 3 student 2. An EVS teacher in a school 3. A swimming coach Critical Thinking

C. Read the text and answer the questions: Veena brought a simple, healthy lunch to school every day. She noticed Lakshmi never had a lunch box and felt sad. Her grandmother said no one should go hungry and encouraged her to help. Veena spoke to her teacher and started a 'Lunch Share Day' where children took turns bringing extra food to share. This helped everyone feel included and supported the idea that good food is every child's right.

1. Is it fair that some children get healthy food and others don't?
2. Are simple, local foods healthy? 3. What steps can you take to reduce food wastage? 4. Do you think we should share our food?

Project and Portfolio

A. Individual activity: Make a diary of foods you like and dislike. Paste or draw pictures of these foods along with the plant or animal they come from. For each food, show how it makes you feel using a word or an emoticon. C-2.1 Creativity

B. Group activity: In groups of five, interview your families and find out about the following:

- Do all members of the family eat the same food?
- Who buys the food and what foodstuffs are bought from the market?
- Who cooks the food in the family?
- Are there any babies at home? What do these babies have for food?

Discuss and make a report using the information collected, in your mother tongue. Present your report in class. C-6.1

C. Interdisciplinary activity: In groups of five, choose any one dish that is most commonly eaten at your homes. Collect data on how the dish is made. With the help of the data, make a label for the dish and give all the information. C-6.2 SI Mathematics

D. Field trip: Take children to visit a nearby farm and discuss with the farmer the type of food he grows, the tools he uses, the problems he faces and how he sells his produce. Make a detailed note and discuss it in class. C-6.2 Collaboration

Self-review

Colour the smileys to show how well you have understood the concepts.	Completely	Mostly	Need help
• I can describe the importance of food for good health.	☺	☺	☺
• I can explain the sources of food.	☺	☺	☺
• I can identify the meals of the day and food requirements of different family members.	☺	☺	☺
• I can identify healthy food and differentiate between fresh and rotten food.	☺	☺	☺
• I can list the various regional dishes of India.	☺	☺	☺

Teacher's Tip

Get some pictures of a few foodstuffs and let the children sort them according to the source, the group they belong to and the nutrients they provide. Ask the children to observe whether they are able to eat food from all the groups.

11 Staying Healthy, Happy and Safe

Learning Outcomes

The learner:

- describes healthy practices for health and safety.
- differentiates between good touch and bad touch.
- discusses how to prepare for emergency situations like fire or injury.
- explains the importance of happiness and well-being.
- describes what is child labour.

Warm-up

Sit calmly in a circle and reflect on each of them. Draw these in your notebook:

- Three things that makes you feel safe and comfortable
- Three things that makes you feel loved
- Three things that made you feel scared

C-3.1

HEALTHY PRACTICES

We should eat healthy food, exercise, rest and think positive thoughts to stay healthy and fit. It is also important to practice safety rules to stay safe at Home, school and on the road. We must take good care of our body and form good and healthy **habits** to stay fit and fine. Some of these are:

- Bathe every day using soap and water, and dry yourself with a clean towel.
- Wash and oil your hair regularly to keep your scalp clean and avoid lice.
- Brush your teeth twice a day to keep them healthy and clean.
- Trim your nails often—long nails can collect germs.
- Wash your hands with soap before and after eating, after using the toilet, and after playing.

We must brush our teeth twice daily.

- Keep your nose clean and use a handkerchief. Always cover your mouth when you cough or sneeze.
- Use clean toilets and flush after use. Leave the toilet floor dry and clean.

My India

Since olden days, people have been using small sticks from trees like neem and babool called *datun*. One end of the stick is used like a toothbrush. The juice from the neem sticks helps to keep the teeth and gums healthy. How is *datun* better than toothpaste?

Health and Diseases

Dirty surroundings can cause diseases and infections. We can stay safe from diseases by keeping our surroundings clean.

- Flies spread diseases such as diarrhoea, cholera and food poisoning. They sit on garbage dumps and dirt. Germs get stuck on their legs. When these flies sit on our food, the germs settle on the food. When we eat this food with germs in it, we fall sick.

Flies on food

- Mosquitoes cause diseases by biting people. Some of the common diseases caused by mosquitoes are malaria, dengue and chikungunya. Mosquitoes breed in water that is stagnant. That is why you should not allow water to collect near your home or in containers. You should keep your surroundings clean.

Water collected in a cooler attracting mosquitoes

Our health, happiness and safety are in our hands. Besides staying healthy, we also need to be careful and stay safe.

SAFE PRACTICES

We should take care of ourselves and stay safe from injury. We can do so, if we follow some safety measures. Let us look at them.

My Eco Club

Throw collected water into plants instead of letting it sit in places where it can attract mosquitoes.

- We should put away our toys and other things after use. Do not litter, else one might trip over them and get hurt.
- We should keep our bathroom floors dry to avoid slippage.
- We should stay away from gas stoves and electric appliances like ovens and toasters, plugs and sharp objects like knives and scissors.

- In our classrooms, we should avoid running around the benches or climbing the chairs.
- Avoid running on stairs and pushing each other on the stairs or swings. Wait for your turn on the swings.
- We should not get on or off a moving vehicle. DO not put your hands or face out while in a moving vehicle.
- We should not play or run on the roads. It is important to walk on the footpaths
- Avoid crossing the road alone. Always cross the road with an elder.
- Follow safety symbols on the roads to avoid accidents and stay safe. Find out what the road signs shown here mean.

By following these rules we can stay safe. Besides these, we should also know how to take care of ourselves with other people, especially strangers.

STAYING SAFE WITH PEOPLE

It is important to know how to keep ourselves safe. A good touch feels nice and safe, like a hug from your parents. A bad touch feels uncomfortable or scary, and it can come from strangers or even someone you know. If someone touches you in a way that feels wrong, even if it seemed okay at first, tell a trusted adult like your parents or teacher. Your safety is very important, and you should always speak up if something feels strange.

Hugs from parents feel safe.

WHAT TO DO IN AN EMERGENCY?

Sometimes, we may get into an emergency even when we are careful. We or someone else may either get hurt or there could be a fire breakout.

In case of fire, we should immediately call 101 and alert the nearest fire station. There are many causes for fire. Sometimes a fire is caused due to an electrical fault. In that case we should never try to put out that fire, using water. Such fires can be put out using sand or special instruments called **fire extinguishers**. We should never play with fire.

Fact Finder

The Uphaar Cinema fire in Delhi was a tragic accident which occured on June 13, 1997, during a movie screening, killing 59 people and injuring over 100. It was caused by an electrical fault. The exits were blocked, which trapped people. This highlights the importance of fire safety and emergency preparedness in public places.

We should give immediate help to anyone who gets injured. The immediate help given to an injured person is called **first aid**.

- If someone gets hurt, we must immediately go to an elder and call for a doctor. Till the doctor arrives, we could clean small cuts and wounds with water and then put an antiseptic cream. Cover the wound with a clean handkerchief or bandage till the doctor arrives

In groups, conduct a **drill** to practically learn first aid tips to follow in emergencies.

For all emergency situations, we must always keep a first aid kit at home as well as in school.

Typically a first aid kit must contain:

- An antiseptic lotion,
- An antiseptic cream,
- Sticking plasters, bandges and gauze
- Sterilized cotton
- Scissor and gloves

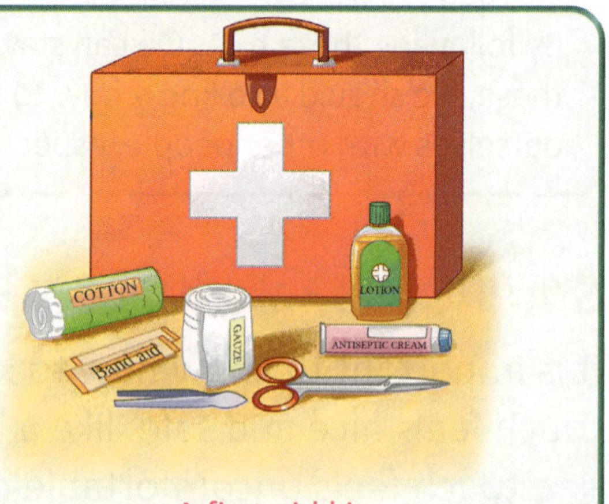

A first aid kit

We go to a doctor when we are ill. A nurse helps take care of the sick and helps them gain good health. An ambulance is a special vehicle that helps to take the sick to a hospital.

OUR HAPPINESS

Our happiness comes from feeling good inside and outside. When we eat healthy food, sleep well and play with friends, we feel happy. Being clean, safe and kind to others also makes us feel good. Helping someone, sharing toys or lunch and saying kind words can bring smiles to everyone. When we are healthy and feel safe, we enjoy each day and feel happy in our hearts.

Activity Corner

Sit cross-legged in a circle on the floor and close your eyes. Stay quiet and still for five minutes while your teacher keeps time. Let your thoughts and feelings come and go. After five minutes, open your eyes gently and draw whatever you felt, thought, or imagined. You can also share your feelings with the class during circle time. Understanding our feelings and being gentle with them helps us stay happy.

CHILD LABOUR

A child working at a tea stall

Many families in our country are poor and do not have enough money. In some of these families, children are unable to go to school because they have to work and earn money for the family. They work as **domestic help**, on farms, in tea stalls and *dhabas*, sell things on streets, and do many such jobs to earn some money. This is known as child labour.

These children are forced to work for long hours in unhealthy places. Child labour harms their bodies and minds. Most of them are not treated well by their employers and are often given less money for the work they do.

It is important to find ways to stop child labour and make the world a happy place for everyone.

Sustainable Development Goals (SDGs)

SDG 8: Decent Work and Economic Growth

Child labour is a problem in many parts of the world. However, in many countries now, it is compulsory for every child to attend school till a certain age, to get basic education. Good schools have been opened so that all children can be educated. Do you think every child should go to school? Make a poster to spread awareness around the ills children face with child labour. Talk about it in class. C-3.3

Our Values

We should help each other in times of need. We should run to call an elder when someone gets hurt.

- Have you ever helped somebody who has got hurt or needs your help?

New Words

Habits: A thing that you do often as routine

Fire extinguishers: Special instruments that can be used to put out fires using sand or chemicals

First aid: The immediate help given to an injured person before help arrives

Drill: A practice of what people must do in order to escape safely from a fire in a building

Domestic help: A person who works in somebody's house, doing the cleaning and other jobs

Let's Remember

Staying Healthy, Happy and Safe

- **Healthy Practices** → We should eat healthy, exercise, rest and think positive thoughts to stay healthy and fit. It is also important to stay in clean surroundings.
- **Safe Practices** → Safety practices help us prevent injury and keep us safe.
- **Staying Safe with People** → Good touch is safe and comfortable. Bad touch is unsafe and uncomfortable.
- **What to Do in an Emergency?** → We should follow fire safety practices in case of a fire. We must give first aid to an injured person before a doctor arrives.
- **Child Labour** → When poor children are forced to work to earn money, it is called child labour.

Exercises

A. Choose the correct answers.

Remembering and Understanding

1. Which of these will help us stay healthy and fit?
   (a) Eating healthy food
   (b) Exercising the body and keeping it clean
   (c) Resting well
   (d) All of these
2. Which of these practices will help you stay clean?
   (a) Washing your hands before and after eating food.
   (b) Washing your hands after going to the toilet.
   (c) Having a bath daily and brush your teeth twice every day.
   (d) All of these.
3. Which of these is not a good touch?
   (a) Something that makes us uncomfortable.
   (b) Something that makes us feel unsafe.

(c) A touch by strangers

(d) All of these

4. Read the statements below and choose the correct option.

   Statement (A): We should keep our body healthy and fit.

   Statement (B): Eating healthy foods and daily exercise helps the body stay healthy.

   (a) Both (A) and (B) are true, and (B) is the correct explanation of (A).

   (b) Both (A) and (B) are true, but (B) is not the correct explanation of (A).

   (c) (A) is true but (B) is false.

   (d) (A) is false but (B) is true.

B. Fill in the blanks.

1. We ______________ (should/should not) keep our bathroom floors dry to avoid slippage.
2. A ______________ (good/bad) touch makes us feel safe and comfortable.
3. We ______________ (should/should not) play with fire.
4. We should use ______________ (water/fire extinguishers) to put out fires caused by electrical faults.
5. Children working to earn money is called ______________. (child labour/ orphans)

C. Give one word for the following.

1. A touch that makes us feel unsafe and uncomfortable: ______________
2. The place where we call to put out fires: ______________
3. Immediate help given to an injured person before help arrives: ______________
4. A box that contains all items of to help an injured person: ______________
5. Something that comes from feeling good inside and out: ______________

D. Answer the following questions.

1. Write five things you do to stay healthy and fit.
2. Write five rules of safety you practice in your daily life.
3. What is a good touch? How is it different from a bad touch?
4. What is first aid? How would you help someone in a fire emergency?
5. What can we do to stay happy?
6. What is child labour? What should we do to prevent child labour?

Reflect and Learn

A. Discuss: How can we help children working in shops or factories around us? Communication

B. Think and Answer: What is more important for children—to earn money or go to school? Why? Critical Thinking

C. Read the text and answer the questions: The Indian government has made education free and compulsory for all children. The Sarva Shiksha Abhiyaan (SSA) is a programme run by the government to help provide free education to children between 6 and 14 years of age. However, many poor children in our country still work in very dangerous places like fireworks industries in Sivakasi (Tamil Nadu) and silk factories in Karnataka.

1. How would programmes like the SSA help children?
2. Why do children need to sometimes work in factories?
3. Do you think it is good for children to work in a fireworks factory?

Project and Portfolio

A. Individual activity: Make a sock puppet and talk about Good Touch Bad touch using the puppet as a model. C-1.5 Creativity

B. Group activity: In groups of five, find out the best ways of taking care of our teeth. Make a simple handout with rules and tips for people to follow and when to seek a dentist. C-1.5 Collaboration

C. Field trip: Visit a fire station and find out how fire fighters work and the kind of equipment they use to put out different kinds of fires. C-3.2

Self-review

Colour the smileys to show how well you have understood the concepts.	Completely	Mostly	Need help
• I can describe healthy practices for health and safety.	☺	☺	☺
• I can differentiate between good touch and bad touch.	☺	☺	☺
• I can discuss how to prepare for emergency situations like fire or injury.	☺	☺	☺
• I can explain the importance of happiness and well-being.	☺	☺	☺
• I can describe what is child labour.	☺	☺	☺

Teacher's Tip

Use age-appropriate language and create a safe, open space for children to ask questions. Reinforce the idea that their body belongs to them and they should always speak up if something feels wrong.

Problem Solving and Life Skills

Chapter 9

Mayank says we can also store rainwater in containers for later use.

1. If you could store rainwater for later use, which of these would you use?
   (a) Tanks and buckets (b) Pots and pans (c) Both (a) and (b)
2. Which of these would you not use stored rainwater for?
   (a) Washing and cleaning clothes
   (b) Watering plants
   (c) Cooking and drinking

Chapter 10

A. Name any three foods that the following people should eat, according to what they do.
   1. A Class 3 student ____________________
   2. A Teacher in a school ____________________
   3. A swimming coach ____________________

B. Give one reason for your choice in each case.
   1. ____________________
   2. ____________________
   3. ____________________

Chapter 11

When we get hurt, we use a special piece of material called a bandage. It helps to cover the cut area and reduce swelling. We should wait for an elder to help us and use a clean bandage.

1. Have you ever seen a bandage? ____________________ (Yes/No)
2. What does it look like?
   (a) A plastic bag (b) A piece of cloth (c) A pencil
3. Complete and write two questions about a bandage starting with:
   (a) What (b) How
4. What can happen if we use a dirty bandage on a cut area?
   (a) It can get better faster.
   (b) The cut area will get spoilt.
   (c) The bandage will tie better.

SHELTERS AROUND THE WORLD

Observing

Circle Time

1. What are the various things that affect the kind of house Jignesh saw in the story?
2. Why do you think some houses are made on sticks?
3. What makes some houses strong, while some are weak?
4. How do you keep your home clean?
5. How different would our life be if we did not live in a house?

12 Our World of Things

Learning Outcomes

The learner:

- classifies things around as transparent, translucent and opaque.
- defines matter and lists the states of matter.
- explains how matter changes its state from one form to another in various ways.
- understands solubility and establishes why water is known as a universal solvent.

Warm-up

Look around the classroom and draw any two things you find in each of the following groups.

Things that have a fixed shape and size	Things that do not have a fixed shape but take the shape of what they are poured into

C-6.1

There are so many things that exist around us. They all seem to be so different to each other. I have often seen that milk comes in a glass bottle and then mother pours it into a bowl to boil. It can easily flow. And then it easily flows into a glass. Isn't that amazing?

It is as though it has no shape. And I am sure we cannot do the same with this book or a pen. I wonder what things are made up of.

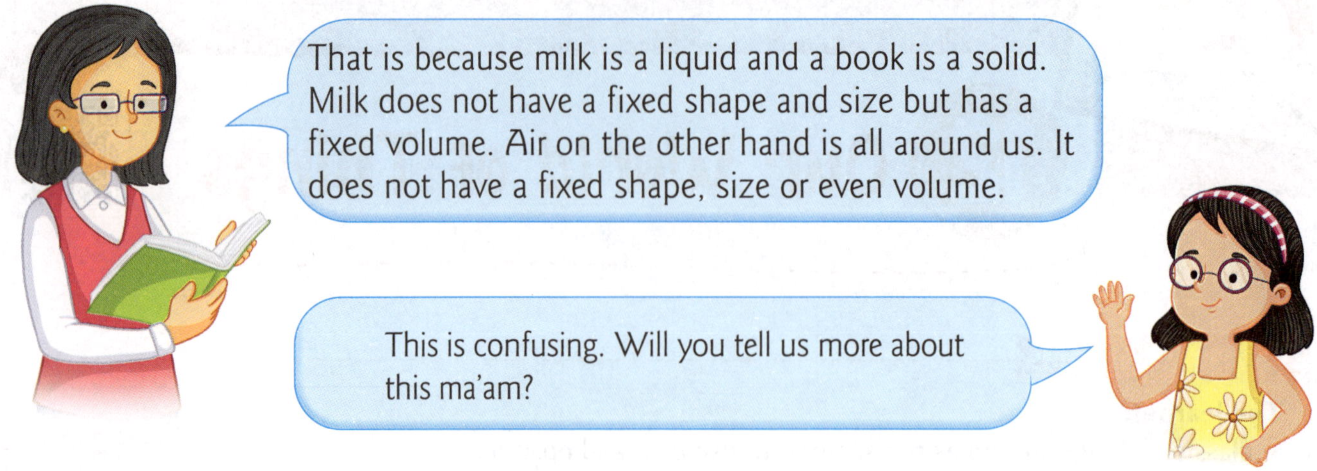

THINGS AROUND US

There are many different kinds of things around us. They are made of a variety of **materials** like paper, cloth, wood, metal, rubber, stone, plastic, clay and even glass.

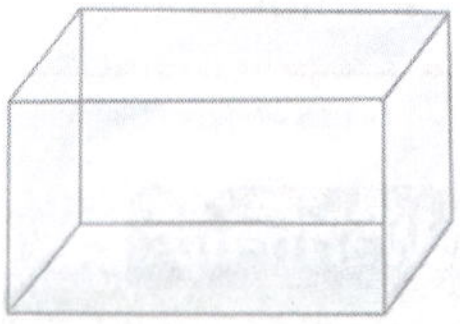

A transparent box

If you closely look at things around you, you can see through some of the things completely, partially through some, while some do not allow you to see through them.

Things that allow you to see through them are called **transparent** things.

A table is opaque.

Things that allow you to partially see through them are called **translucent** things.

Things that do not let us see through them, are called **opaque** objects.

Activity Corner

C-7.1

Walk around the classroom with a pencil. Try banging any five things with it, in class and observe the difference in sound.
Name these things and arrange them in order from loudest sound to softest sound.

Loudest Thing				Softest Thing

Now use the same pencil to push through paper and your study table. What did you observe? ______________________

Is it easier to push the pencil through paper or wood? ______________________

MATTER

A chair is a solid

Things are made up of particles. These particles join together to form different things. All that exists around us is called **matter**. Matter is made up of particles. The manner in which particles are arranged makes things fall into three main groups or states:

(i) Solids (ii) Liquids (iii) Gas

Let us look at each of them.

Solids

Some things, like books, pencils, and tables, have a fixed shape and size, depending on how they are made. These things do not change their shape when packed into containers. They are called solids. Particles inside solids are tightly packed and thus solids have a fixed shape and size.

Liquids

Liquids take the shape of the container they are in.

Things like water, oil, and milk do not have a fixed shape. They flow easily and take the shape of the container they are poured in. Such things are called liquids.

Particles in liquids are a little far apart than solids but are still not very very far like in gases. This is why liquids do not have a fixed shape but take the shape of the container. They do have a fixed **volume** though. Example, milk in a bottle is 1 litre. Even though it is poured into a bowl, the volume remains 1 litre though the shape changes.

Gases

Matter with no shape, size or volume of its own is called a gas. Like liquids, gases can also flow. Air, Water vapour or steam, oxygen and carbon dioxide are examples of a gas. Particles are very far apart in gases. The air we breathe is a mixture of many gases.

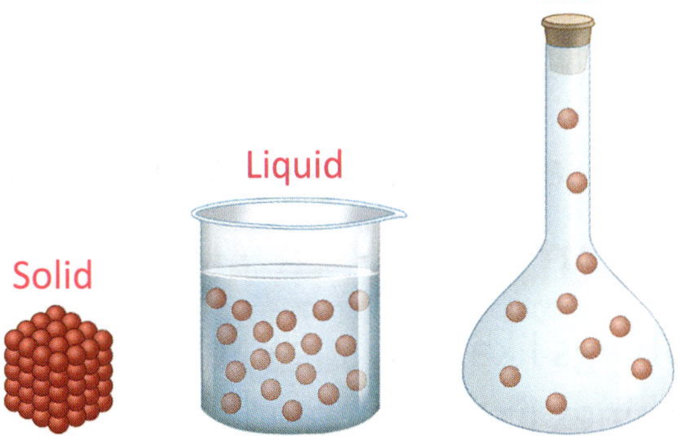

Particles in a solid, liquid and gas

All living things need oxygen to live. Let us look at the three states of matter again.

Solids	Liquids	Gases
Fixed shape	No fixed shape	No fixed shape
Fixed Size	No Fixed size	No Fixed Size
Fixed Volume	Fixed Volume	No Fixed Volume

Changes in Matter

Matter changes its state when heated or cooled. Let us look at it using water.

When water is cooled to a certain temperature, water freezes to form ice, and the process is called freezing or solidification.

Ice, when left outside melts due to heat, and changes its state from solid to liquid. This process by which a solid changes into a liquid due to heat is called melting.

When water is boiled, it changes its state from a liquid to a gas after some time. This process by which water changes to vapour is called evaporation and the gaseous form of water is called water vapour.

Condensation on a window

When water vapour cools down, it changes back to liquid water. This process by which water vapour changes to water on cooling is called condensation.

Thus, water can change from one form to another by heating or cooling. In nature, this change in the states of water gives us rain.

Be a Scientist

Add 1 teaspoon of sugar in a glass of tap water and mix well. Where does sugar disappear after sometime? ________________

What would happen if you add 1 teaspoon of salt in water?

Now add 1 teaspoon of sand in a glass of tap water. Mix well and leave it for 10 minutes.

What happens to the sand? _______________

What does this indicate? ___________________________ C-7.1

Now let us see what happens when we add things to water.

SOLUTE, SOLVENT AND SOLUTION

Things like salt, sugar, milk dissolve in water and are called **soluble** substances. Things like sand, mud, grass etc do not dissolve in water and are called **insoluble** substances.

When a soluble substance like salt dissolves in water, then the salty water that gets formed is called a **solution**. The water in which the salt dissolves is called the **solute**.

Salt + Water	= Salty water
(Solute) + (Solvent)	= Solution

Sedimentation and decantation process

Most things dissolve in water and therefore water is also known as a universal **solvent.**

We can remove insoluble substances from water through simple processes like:

(i) Sedimentation

(ii) Decantation

(iii) Filtration

Filtration

Though these processes can help in removing insoluble substances from water, we need different processes to remove soluble substances from water.

If you leave salty water out in the sun, what would happen? ____________________________

The water will change into vapour and evaporate due to the heat of the sun and salt would be left behind.

My Eco Club

Much water gets wasted when taps leaks. We should get them fixed.

Fact Finder

There are many things like oils, and wax that do not dissolve in water. Though water is called a universal solvent, many things do not dissolve in it. Place half cup of vinegar and half a cup of oil in a bottle, and shake it in the bottle and leave it for 15 minutes. Observe and see what happens. C-7.1

Sustainable Development Goals (SDGs)

Goal 14: Life Below Water

Oil spills harm sea animals and plants by polluting the water and making it hard for them to breathe and grow. Keeping oceans clean helps protect life under water. Draw a picture showing clean ocean life and another showing how oil spills affect fish, turtles, and plants. Then talk about how we can help keep oceans clean.

Our Values

We must avoid using materials made of plastic, especially for storing food.

- How can you replace plastic materials in your home?

Keywords

Materials: A substance that things can be made from

Transparent: Material that allows us to see through them fully

Translucent: Material that allows us to see through them partially

Opaque: Material that do not allow us to see through them

Matter: Physical material that everything is made of

Volume: The amount of space that an object or a substance fills; the amount of space that a container has

Soluble: Substances that dissolve in water

Insoluble: Substances that do not dissolve in water

Solute: Substance that dissolves in a liquid to form a solution

Solvent: Substance that dissolves the solute.

Solution: The result formed when a solute dissolves in a solvent

Let's Remember

Our World of Things

- **Things around Us** → Things are transparent (see-through), translucent (partially see-through) or opaque (cannot see through at all).
- **Matter** → Matter has three states: Solids (tightly held particles), liquids (loose particles) and gases (very loose particles).
- **Changes in Matter** → Matter changes its state when heated or cooled. Water freezes on cooling, melts on heating and becomes vapour on boiling.
- **Solute, Solvent and Solution** → Things like salt and milk are solvents. Water is a solvent. Salt mixed in water forms a solution. Water is a universal solvent.

Exercises

A. Choose the correct answers.

Remembering and Understanding

1. Which of these has the particles very closely packed?
   (a) Book
   (b) Ink
   (c) Water
   (d) Air
2. Which of these is not true about liquids?
   (a) They have a fixes shape and size.
   (b) They do not have a fixed volume.
   (c) They cannot flow.
   (d) All of these.
3. Mohan put water in an ice tray and put it in the freezer. What can you expect would happen?
   (a) Water will boil and change to vapour.
   (b) Water will freeze and become ice.
   (c) Water will melt to change to vapour.
   (d) Water will melt to change into ice.
4. Which of these is true about a solvent?
   (a) It always dissolves in water.
   (b) It is insoluble.
   (c) It dissolves a solute to form a solution.
   (d) It freezes to form ice.
5. Read the statements below and choose the correct option.
   Statement (A): Solids, liquids and gases are made up of particles.
   Statement (B): Particles are arranged in different ways.
   (a) Both (A) and (B) are true, and (B) is the correct explanation of (A).
   (b) Both (A) and (B) are true, but (B) is not the correct explanation of (A).
   (c) (A) is true but (B) is false. (d) (A) is false but (B) is true.

B. Fill in the blanks.

1. All matter is made up of ______________. (solids/particles)
2. Particles are ______________ (tightly packed/very far away) in a gas.

3. ________ (Liquids/Solids) flow.

4. When water is heated, it changes into __________ (ice/water vapour) and the process is called __________ (evaporation/condensation)

5. When ice is _________ (cooled/heated), it changes into water.

6. Water is called a universal ____________. (solution/solvent)

C. Give one word for each of the following.

1. Things around us made of particles:___________
2. State of matter in which particles are very tightly packed:___________
3. The process by which water changes to vapour:___________
4. Substances that do not dissolve in water:___________
5. The substance in which a solute dissolves:___________

D. Answer the following questions.

1. What are transparent, translucent and opaque things?
2. Differentiate between a solid, liquid and a gas with two examples of each.
3. Define evaporation. How is it different from freezing?
4. With the help of an example, explain a solute, solvent and solution.
5. Which processes help us remove insoluble substances from water?

Reflect and Learn

21st CENTURY SKILLS

A. Discuss: How does heating or cooling affect the state of matter? Communication

B. Think and Answer: How will you distinguish between the different things depending upon the particles they are made of? Critical Thinking

C. Read the text and answer the questions: On a cold winter morning, Riya noticed that she could clearly see through the glass window, but only partly through the frosted glass on the door. She could not see anything through the wooden cupboard. She also noticed tiny droplets of water on the glass of the window.

1. Classify the glass window, frosted glass, and wooden cupboard as transparent, translucent, or opaque.
2. Where do you think water droplets on the window came from?

Project and Portfolio

A. Individual activity: Go to the kitchen and make a list of all the liquids being used there. Draw them using colours as symbols. C-7.1 C-7.2 SI Arts Education

B. Group activity: In groups of five, make any three different kinds of solutions. Explain the solute, solvent and solution in each and how stirring and warmer temperature helped in dissolving the solute. Describe your observations in your own word. C-7.1 C-7.2 Collaboration

C. Interdisciplinary activity: Draw pictures to show how particles are arranged in a solid, liquid and gas. Then use straws and play-doh to show the structures as a model. C-7.1 C-7.2 SI Arts Education

D. Field trip: Visit the water plant of the town or city you live in and observe how water is purified before it is sent to our homes. Observe the process of filtration or sedimentation and decantation involved and then prepare a report C-7.1 C-7.2 SI Science

Self-review

Colour the smileys to show how well you have understood the concepts.	Completely	Mostly	Need help
• I can classify things around as transparent, translucent and opaque.	☺	☺	☺
• I can define matter and list the states of matter.	☺	☺	☺
• I can explain how matter changes its state from one form to another in various ways.	☺	☺	☺
• I can understand solubility and establish why water is known as a universal solvent.	☺	☺	☺

Teacher's Tip

Let the children talk about the things they see in their classroom and classify them into transparent, translucent and opaque, or solids, liquids and gases. You could also get some ice cubes and show changes in the states of matter.

13 Things We Make and Do

Learning Outcomes

The learner:

- identifies the types of houses and how they are built according to location.
- describes how clothes are made and dyed.
- explains how pottery was made by early humans.
- describes the method of making pottery and cites everyday examples of use.

Warm-up

Observing

Colour the various things made out of clay that are being used in Yash and Shriya's house.

I wonder why people make a house ? Why can't we live under the sky? Did people always live in houses?

Daddy says, a house helps us stay safe from heat, cold and even wild animals

People in olden times lived in caves and even under trees and on trees as well. Then, people learnt how to make bricks and use them to make houses. These houses help us stay safe. People make a variety of houses.

HOUSES WE MAKE

We can divide houses into different types based on the following features.

- The materials available and the cost of building houses
- The location where houses are built
- Temporary and permanent houses

Houses Based on Materials Used

Based on the materials used, houses can be divided into two types—kuchcha houses and pucca houses. Let us learn about them.

Kuchcha Houses

A kuchcha house

Houses that are made of mud, straw, bamboo sticks and reeds are known as kuchcha houses. The roofs of these houses are made of thatched straw, palm leaves or tin sheets. These houses are not very strong and at times strong winds can damage them. People living in villages and poor people in cities live in kuchcha houses. The materials used to make kuchcha houses do not cost a lot of money.

Pucca Houses

A pucca house

Strong houses made of bricks, cement, steel and mortar are called pucca houses. All bungalows, single **storey** and multi-storey houses as well as tall apartment buildings are pucca houses. The materials used to make these houses cost more money than those used for kuchcha houses.

Houses Based on Location

There are some special kinds of houses that are found in particular areas. The kind of house built in a place depends upon the climate of the place and the materials available to build the house.

Fact Finder

Thatched roofs are made of natural materials that can last for a long time. However, you need to replace it regularly. But thatched roofs can keep the insides of the house cool. Find out how thatched roofs can be adapted as an eco-friendly option in city homes too. C-1.1

A house on stilts

In hilly areas or in the mountains, where it rains or snows a lot, houses are built with sloping roofs. This helps rainwater or snow to slide off the roofs to the ground.

In the plains, houses are mostly built with flat roofs.

In places where it rains a lot, people make houses on poles called stilts. They do this to protect themselves from standing water, snakes, insects and wild animals. Some places in the north-eastern part of India have houses on stilts.

Houses that are built on boats and float on water are known as houseboats. Such houses are commonly seen on the Dal Lake in Srinagar in Kashmir and in the backwaters of Kerala.

A house on stilts

Sustainable Development Goals (SDGs)

Goal 11: Sustainable Cities and Communities

Long ago, people in India built homes using natural materials like mud, clay, cow dung, and straw. Cow dung mixed with mud made strong walls, kept insects away, and helped homes stay cool in summer and warm in winter. Windows were placed opposite each other to let air flow and keep rooms fresh without fans. Why do you think people used cow dung and mud in their homes? (C-1.1)

CLOTHES WE WEAR

Early humans used the bark of trees, leaves and animal skins to cover themselves and to stay warm. Later, they wore clothes made by **sewing** animal skins together. Over a period of time, they learnt the art of **spinning fibres** such as cotton, silk, jute and wool into threads and weaving the threads into cloth.

Now, people wear a variety of clothes made from different materials, with different colours and designs. The main factors that determine what people wear are:

- The climate of the place where people live
- The culture and tradition
- The price of clothes
- The latest fashion and trends

Let us learn how clothes are made.

A frock made from cotton

How Clothes Are Made

The clothes we wear are made of different materials. They have different colours, patterns and designs on them. A cloth is made from different types of fibres. The two ways of making cloth from fibres are weaving and knitting.

Weaving

Weaving is the process of making cloth on special machines called looms. Two sets of threads are woven together on a loom to form cloth. Looms are of two types—those which are operated by hand and those that run on power . Saris, your school uniform, pants, shirts, and many other clothes are all made out of woven cloth.

Weaving

Knitting

This is a simple process of making cloth. It can be done by hand using two thin knitting needles or by machines. Socks, sweaters, swimsuits and T shirts are some clothes made from knitted cloth.

Colouring the Cloth

Sometimes threads are coloured before the cloth is woven or knitted, while at other times, the cloth is made first and then coloured or dyed. Dyeing is the process of colouring the cloth by soaking it in a coloured solution. This solution is made of water and dyes.

A dye is a substance that is used to change the colour of cloth. Dyes are of two kinds—vegetable dyes and chemical dyes. Vegetable dyes are natural colours that we get from flowers, fruits, vegetables and other parts of plants.

Natural fabric dye

Designs on Clothes

Patterns and designs are made on cloth to make it look beautiful. There are several ways to do so.

1. Threads of different colours are woven together into one cloth. They are woven in such a way that they create a design on the cloth.
2. Designs are painted on a cloth after the cloth is woven.
3. Designs can be **embroidered** on a cloth using a needle and coloured threads. Embroidery can be done by hand or by using a machine. Nowadays, computerized embroidery machines are also available.
4. Designs can also be printed on cloth. There are two kinds of printing—screen printing and block printing:
   (a) In screen printing, designs are made on screens and then printed on a cloth using colours. Screen printing can be done by hand or by machines.
   (b) In block printing, designs are carved on wooden blocks, which are dipped in dye and then pressed on a cloth. Block printing is done by hand and is much more costly than screen printing.

Block printing

There are some other methods of making designs on cloth which are popular in different parts of India.

Activity Corner

Bring a *dupatta* or a shawl from your home to your classroom. Look at it closely and find out the following. • Is it woven or knitted cloth? • What colour is it dyed in? • Does it have any designs? • Identify the kind of design(s) making process used. (C-4.2)

POTTERY

Early human making earthen pot

Once early humans learnt how to make their food, shelter and clothes, there was a need for vessels to store their food. That is how they started using a type of soil called **clay** to make vessels. They used their hands to shape the clay and then rolled it into strips. The strips were joined together to make vessels, which were then dried in the sun.

However, people discovered that water could not be stored in these vessels because they would break. Soon people learnt that baking their clay vessels in fire would make them stronger. Water could be stored in these baked vessels. With the invention of the potter's wheel, people could make pots of various shapes and sizes much faster. They often decorated their pots with beautiful designs and patterns. This led to the art of pottery.

My India

Long, long ago people in the Indus Valley civilization in India made pots using mud and their hands. Pots were used to store water, grains, and even cook food. These pots were decorated with simple patterns by drawing shapes and simple things around them like animals, leaves, sun, moon and stars. How were pots being used by early humans?

The Art of Pottery

Pottery is considered as one of the oldest forms of art. Pottery refers to the objects made of clay, which are baked in an oven to make them stronger. Clay is soft soil which becomes sticky when wet and can be moulded into different shapes. After clay is shaped, it is baked in special ovens to make it strong. Pots, jars, vases, diyas, bowls and dishes are some examples.

How to Make Pottery

Pottery is a step-by-step process. Its steps are described below.

1. The first step to do pottery is to choose the right clay. Sometimes potters add other things like husk, ash, chalk or sand to make the clay better for pottery.
2. Then water is added, just enough so that the potter is able to **knead** the clay well and make it into a lump.
3. After this, the clay is shaped into different objects such as pots and bowls.
4. Once the objects are shaped, they are baked in fire.
5. In the end, the pottery is decorated.

Kneading the clay

How Clay Is Shaped

There are various methods of shaping clay. Let us study two of the most common ones below.

1. The hand-building method
2. The wheel method

Hand-building method is very simple and does not involve a wheel. In this method, the clay is pressed and shaped by hand. There are three kinds of hand-building methods.

1. Coiling, shaping the clay into long coils. These coils are placed over one another in a round shape to form different objects.
2. Slab building, or rolling out the clay into flat slabs. These are then joined together to make containers.
3. Press moulding, or pressing the clay inside or over a mould of desired shape: The clay then takes the shape of the **mould**. The art of making pottery on a potter's wheel is very common.

The coiling method

The potter's wheel is a flat, round, wooden or metal surface. In the wheel method, a potter places a lump of kneaded clay on the wheel. The potter then makes the wheel spin either by using a stick or by pushing it with the feet.

My Eco Club

Using articles made of clay is environment-friendly. Keeping drinking water in clay pots also keeps the water cool.

Nowadays, motorized wheels are also available. While the wheel spins, the potter gives shape to the clay, using the hands and fingers. Once the clay is shaped into a pot, the potter cuts off the base of the pot from the clay lump on the wheel. Then, the wet pot is kept aside to dry. When the pottery is ready, it is baked in special ovens called **kilns** to make it hard and strong.

Decorating Pottery

A glazed clay pot

Pottery can be made attractive by decorating it in different ways. It can be painted or glazed. Glazing means covering pottery with a special liquid before baking it. This makes the pottery smooth and shiny after it is baked. It also makes pottery waterproof.

Pottery In Our Daily Life

A pot being used for cooking

Early humans used pottery for storing water and grains. They also used it for cooking, eating and storing water. In many houses even today, people use utensils made of clay for different purposes. Big clay vessels are used to make curd and to store water. Tea is often served in kulhads or clay cups at railway stations. Several toys are made of clay for children. Plants are also grown in clay pots.

Our Values

Many people work very hard to make items of daily use, the clothes that we wear. We should respect their work.

- How many different kinds of work are needed to make one item of clothing that you wear?

Let's Remember

Things We Make and Do

- **Houses We Make**
  - Based on materials used, houses are kuchcha and pucca.
  - Houses change according to location, for example, houseboats and houses on stilts.
- **Clothes We Wear**
  - Weaving and knitting are two ways to make clothes.
  - Clothes are coloured using dyes.
  - Designs are made on clothes using various methods.
- **Pottery**
  - it is a step-by-step process and involves two methods: hand-building methods and wheel method.
  - Early humans used pots to store water and grains. Nowadays, clay vessels are used to make curd, cooking, storing and serving tea.

Keywords

Storey: A floor or a level of a building

Sewing: Using a needle and thread to join pieces of material together

Spinning: Making thread from fibres like wool or cotton by twisting them

Fibres: Thin threads that form materials like wool and cotton

Embroidered: Patterns sewn on cloth with thread

Clay: A kind of heavy soil that becomes hard when baked

Knead: To press and stretch dough, wet clay, etc. with your hands to make it ready for use

Mould: A container into which you put a soft substance, which then dries in the same shape as the container

Kiln: A large oven for baking clay and brick, drying wood and grain, etc.

Exercises

Remembering and Understanding

A. Choose the correct answers.

1. Which of these features affect the kinds of houses we make?
   (a) Materials (b) Cost (c) Location (d) All of these
2. Which of these is the process by which socks are made?
   (a) Weaving (b) Knitting (c) Printing (d) All of these
3. Which of these is done just after we have shaped our clay?
   (a) Kneading the clay (b) Making a lump (c) Baking (d) Decorating
4. Which of these is a hand building method of making pottery?
   (a) Coiling (b) Slab building (c) Press moulding (d) All of these
5. Read the statements below and choose the correct option.
   Statement (A): A pucca house is a strong house.
   Statement (B): A pucca house is made of cement, steel and mortar.
   (a) Both (A) and (B) are true, and (B) is the correct explanation of (A).
   (b) Both (A) and (B) are true, but (B) is not the correct explanation of (A).
   (c) (A) is true but (B) is false. (d) (A) is false but (B) is true.

B. Match the rows.

1. Sari	2. Vegetable dye	3. Cloth	4. Printing	5. Embroidery
(a) Needle and thread	(b) Block and Screen	(c) Fibres	(d) Weaving	(e) Plants

C. Fill in the blanks.

1. Houses that are built on boats and float on water are known as ____________. (houseboats/tent)
2. Wearing clothes depends on the ____________ of the place we live in. (vegetation/climate)
3. ____________ is the process of colouring the cloth. (painting/dyeing)
4. Coiling is a ____________ method of shaping clay. (hand-building/wheel)
5. The ____________ of the potter's wheel is used to create shapes from a lump of clay. (spinning/surfing)

D. Answer the following questions.

1. How is a temporary house different from a permanent house?
2. What are the various ways in which cloth is made?
3. What are the two kinds of dyes used for colouring cloth?
4. What is pottery? Why is clay used to make pottery?
5. Why do we bake pottery?
6. What is glazing?
7. Describe the step-by-step process of making pottery.
8. Differentiate between printing and embroidery for decorating cloth.

Reflect and Learn

21st CENTURY SKILLS

A. Discuss: How did the invention of pottery make life easier for early humans? Communication

B. Think and Answer: Why is clay better for making pottery than sand? Critical Thinking

C. Read the text and answer the questions: There are some other methods of making designs on cloth which are popular in different parts of India, like *batik*. This is done by pouring molten wax on some parts of a cloth, before dyeing it. After dyeing the cloth, the wax is also removed from it. *Batik* is very popular in West Bengal and some other states of India.

1. What is *batik* and how is it done?
2. How is wax useful in the *batik* method before dyeing the cloth?
3. In which part of India is *batik* especially popular?

D. Look at the picture and answer the questions:

1. What is shown here?
2. How is it done?
3. Is it cheap or costly?

Project and Portfolio

A. Individual activity: Using modelling clay, make one clay article using each of the three hand-building methods. Then dry and paint it. You could make different objects such as a pen stand, a bowl, a cup, a photo frame or a piggy bank. (C-6.2) Creativity SI Arts Education

B. Group activity: In groups of five, collect small samples of any 10 fabrics found at home and paste them in your scrapbook. Identify whether each of them is woven or knitted, the kind of dyeing done, and whether it is printed or embroidered. (C-4.7) Collaboration

C. Interdisciplinary: Find out what a tent or a caravan is. Imagine if you were living in a tent or caravan. What kind of issues would you face in living like this? Write an imaginative account of the life you would live in such a home. (C-6.1) SI English

D. Field/Outdoor: Visit a potter in groups, observe how they use the wheel, and ask about their work and challenges. Discuss how potters live and create a poster to raise awareness. Share your poster and findings with the class. (C-6.1) Problem Solving

Self-review

Colour the smileys to show how well you have understood the concepts.	Completely	Mostly	Need help
• I can identify the types of houses and how they are built according to location.	☺	☺	☺
• I can describe how clothes are made and dyed.	☺	☺	☺
• I can explain how pottery was made by early humans.	☺	☺	☺
• I can describe the method of making pottery and cite everyday examples of use.	☺	☺	☺

Teacher's Tip

Get a slab of modelling clay to class for each child to try their hands on. Let them observe how water helps in kneading and moulding, and also how wet clay is sticky and can be pressed and shaped easily. Allow them to make any one article of daily use and leave it in the sun to dry. Discuss the observations.

14 Mapping

Learning Outcomes

The learner:

- understands what mental maps are and how directions play an important role in our lives.
- explains the importance of maps and some of their elements.
- draws and explains a sketch and line drawing of their school and neighbourhood.
- reads a simple map with reference to some symbols and directions.

Warm-up

Look at the map and answer the questions given. Critical Thinking

1. Which place will you reach if you walk to the right of the house?
2. Where would you reach if you turned left from the house?

We need clear directions to move from one place to another. We use maps to find our way.

MAPPING

A drawing of a place on a flat surface, such as paper, is called a map. The picture given above is a simple map of a neighbourhood. Maps are drawn using exact **measurements** of a place.

Mental Maps

We use simple mental maps to move from one place to another. A mental map is like the mental picture of a place that is kept in our mind. We use mental maps to find our way to the toilet, to our bedroom and even our kitchen.

- Can you draw and make the way from your classroom to the school gate?
- List the places that you would draw on this map. C-5.2

Parts of a Map

Symbols and colours are used to show different things on a map. We make a **legend** or a key to understand what each symbol in a map stands for.

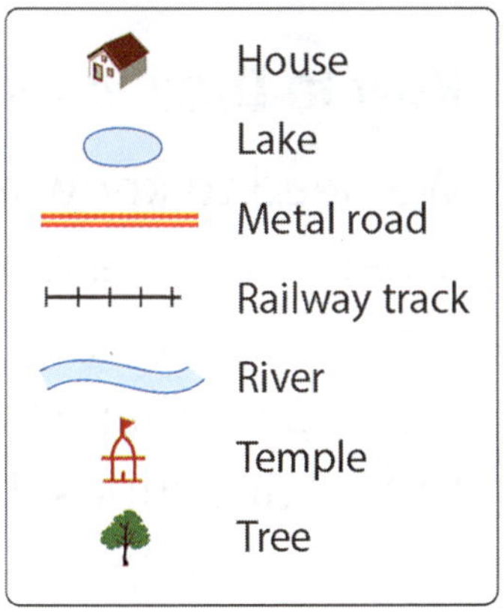

A legend

We usually use different colours to show different kinds of places—green for forests and trees, blue for water bodies and brown for mountains.

A map is much smaller than the actual place it shows. Therefore, it is drawn in such a way that it can be measured to find out the actual size of the place. This is why maps are drawn to scale.

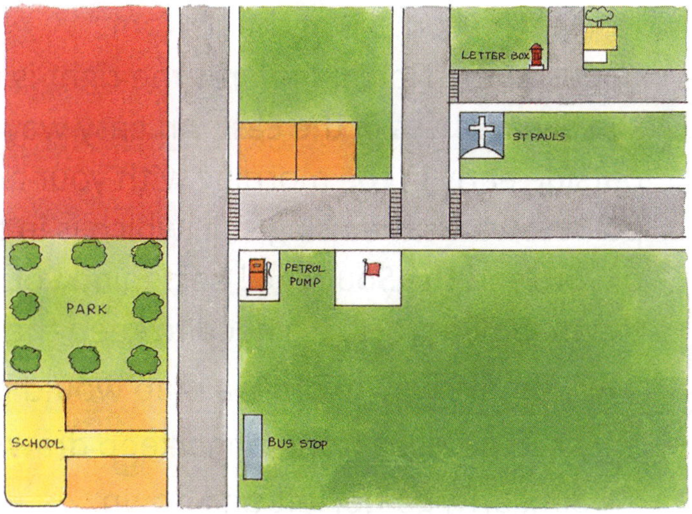

A sketch

A map scale tells you the actual size of a place on the ground or the actual distance between two places on the ground, when these are compared to their sizes or distances on the map. For instance, if the scale says that 1 cm on a map shows 1 km on the ground, then a distance of 5 cm between two places on a map shows an actual distance of 5 km.

Maps that show details of a smaller area like a room, a building or a section of a house, are called plans. When people make their houses, they need to get the plans of their houses made before getting them built.

A rough drawing of a place is called a sketch. It does not have exact measurements. It has symbols, signs or labels showing different landmarks.

A landmark is an important place or a thing that one can easily recognize, such as post offices, schools, hospitals, petrol pumps, police stations, etc. Landmarks help us to know where we are and to find places that are located near them.

Fact Finder

A book of maps is called an atlas. Nowadays people use digital maps and can share their exact location through their devices. Find out how they help.

Activity Corner

In your notebook, draw a map of your classroom. Start with a centre point, such as the teacher's desk or the blackboard. Then go left, right, up and down the classroom and keep adding landmarks on each side.

How to Draw a Map

We need to know about directions in order to draw a map. There are four main directions—North, South, East and West. A compass is an instrument that helps us to find directions. Its needle always points towards the North.

On a map, the top always shows the North. The South is at the bottom, opposite the North. Towards the right is the East and to the left is the West. The sun always rises in the East. An easy way to find the four directions is to stand outside early in the morning with your arms outstretched. Your right hand should point towards the rising sun, which is in the East. Then the North will be in front of you, and the South will be behind you, the West will be to your left. To draw the map of a place, we need to keep the landmarks of that place in mind.

- A simple way to draw a map would be to first take a centre point.
- Then go right from it and keep drawing or marking the landmarks you find.
- Similarly, go up, left and down.
- Use symbols to show each place that you see.
- Then draw a legend to explain the symbols you have used in your map.

Maps are very useful for pilots and sailors. They can keep track of their positions in the air and in the water by looking at maps. We will never lose our way if we learn to read directions and maps well.

My Eco Club

When we use a map to plan our trips, we tend to save time, fuel, and energy. Using a map to find the safest and shortest route can help us save fuels.

Maps are very useful for pilots and sailors. They can keep track of their positions in the air and in the water by looking at maps. We will never lose our way if we learn to read directions and maps well.

My India

The Survey of India is the country's oldest scientific department, set up in 1767. It makes maps that help us understand land, roads, rivers, and boundaries across India. How did people find their way in olden times?

Sustainable Development Goals (SDGs)

Goal 15: Life on Land

Maps help us understand where forests, rivers, mountains, and villages are located. Learning to read maps can help children appreciate nature and understand how to care for the land around them.

Our Values

It is important to give clear directions to people and not confuse them.

- Have you ever given people simple ways to reach your home?

Let's Remember

Mapping

- **Mental Maps**
  - A mental map is like the mental picture of a place that is kept in our mind.
- **Parts of a map**
  - Legend: Explains the symbols used in a map.
  - Scale: Explains the actual size of the ground.
  - Plans show details of a smaller area.
  - Sketch is a rough drawing.
- **Drawing a map**
  - Directions should be mentioned on top.
  - Important landmarks should be marked and symbols used.

Keywords

Measurements: The size, weight or length of something

Legend: The explanation of the colours, signs and symbols in a map

Exercises

A. Choose the correct answers.

Remembering and Understanding

1. Which of these is needed to draw a map of your neighbourhood?
   (a) Knowing directions (b) Symbols to show landmarks
   (c) A legend to explain symbols (d) All of these
2. Which of these is a detailed drawing of a small place like a room or a house?
   (a) Map (b) Plan (c) Legend (d) None of these
3. Which of these show what a neighbourhood school looks like on the map?
   (a) Direction (b) Legend (c) Landmark (d) All of these
4. Which direction is always at the top of a map?
   (a) North (b) West (c) South (d) East

5. Read the statements below and choose the correct option.
   Statement (A): A map helps us find locations of a place.
   Statement (B): A legend has symbols that tell us what each stands for in a map.
   (a) Both (A) and (B) are true, and (B) is the correct explanation of (A).
   (b) Both (A) and (B) are true, but (B) is not the correct explanation of (A).
   (c) (A) is true but (B) is false. (d) (A) is false but (B) is true.

B. Match the rows.

1. Map	2. Plan	3. Sketch	4. Legend	5. Landmark
(a) A map of a smaller area	(b) Rough drawing	(c) List of symbols	(d) An important place	(e) Drawing of a place

C. State whether true or false true or false. Rewrite the false statements correctly.

1. Maps are drawn using the exact measurements of a place.
2. We use symbols to show places on a map.
3. A legend shows the relation between the size of a place on a map and its actual size on the ground.
4. A landmark is an important place or thing that one can easily recognize.
5. Directions are not important in a map.

D. Answer the following questions.

1. What is a map?
2. What is a legend? How is it useful?
3. What is a scale?
4. How is a plan different from a map?
5. Explain how maps are useful to pilots and sailors.

Reflect and Learn

21st CENTURY SKILLS

A. Discuss: What will happen if we did not use a scale to draw a map? Communication

B. Think and Answer:

- What will happen if maps are drawn using only a single colour?
- Do you think it is a better idea to draw symbols without a legend? Justify your answer. Critical Thinking

C. Read the passage and answer the following questions: In ancient times, maps were not just lines but were used to tell stories of how people lived, moved, and connected with the world. In olden times, elders in the village shared the locations of forests, rivers, and hills through stories and symbols or used the position of stars to travel. In coastal areas, fishermen made simple drawings on palm leaves and temple walls to tell people where fish was going to be found or where the shores were safe during storms.

1. What did people use to draw maps in olden days?
2. Why did people need maps in olden times?
3. Why did people use storytelling as a method of telling people locations?

Project and Portfolio

A. Individual activity: Draw a map of the route from your house to the nearest market on a chart paper and give oral directions. C-5.2 SI Geography

B. Group activity: In groups of five, select and draw a map of any of these places:
- Your classroom
- From the classroom to the playground
- From the classroom to the main gate
- From the classroom to the library
- From the library to the staff room

C-5.2 SI Geography

C. Interdisciplinary activity: Imagine yourself as a guide who has to help your friend reach you house from the nearest park. Try and write guided instructions to give clear directions. C-5.3 Creativity

Self-review

Colour the smileys to show how well you have understood the concepts.	Completely	Mostly	Need help
• I can understand what mental maps are and how directions play an important role in our lives.	☺	☺	☺
• I can explain the importance of maps and some of their elements.	☺	☺	☺
• I can draw and explain a sketch and line drawing of their school and neighbourhood.	☺	☺	☺
• I can read a simple map with reference to some symbols and directions.	☺	☺	☺

Teacher's Tip

Help the children understand directions first. Perhaps you could take them out in the morning and help them understand the four main directions. You can also bring a compass to class and show them how the needle always aligns itself in such a way as to point to the north.

15 How We Travel and Communicate

Learning Outcomes

The learner:

- identifies and differentiates between the different modes of transport of the present and the past.
- explains means of communication at home/school/neighbourhood.
- describes occupations in transport and communication.

Warm-up

Read the paragraph below and answer the questions.

Ali and his family were going from Delhi to Bengaluru by air to attend the wedding of Ali's cousin. They left their home early in the morning by car to reach the airport. On reaching Bengaluru, they hired an autorickshaw to the cousin's house. After the wedding, they returned to Delhi by train. It was a great experience for Ali and his sister.

1. How many different ways of travel did Ali and his family use?
2. Name the different vehicles they took. Which was the fastest among them? C-2.1

People travel from one place to another for different reasons. They travel to their places of work. Children go to school. People go to places close to their houses and sometimes to places far away for holidays. They go to malls, shopping centres and other places for other recreational activities. They go to meet friends and relatives and to attend other social events. They also travel to transport goods from one place to another.

MEANS OF TRANSPORT

Means of transport are **vehicles** that help us to move people and goods from one place to another. People use different means of **transport** to travel. Some of these are slow and some are fast. Some move on land, some move in the air and some move on water.

On Land

Vehicles such as cycles, rickshaws, autorickshaws, scooters, motorcycles,

A bicycle

A car

cars, trucks, vans, buses, trams and trains move on land. They are known as means of land transport. Trains and trams move on special tracks made for them.

On Water

Vehicles such as boats, **steamers**, yachts and ships that sail on water are means of water transport.

A ship

In Air

Vehicles such as hot-air balloons, gliders, aeroplanes, helicopters and rockets that move in the air are means of air transport.

An aeroplane

Special Vehicles

There are many special kinds of vehicles that are used for a particular purpose. You may have also seen them.

An ambulance

- Ambulance: An ambulance is a vehicle that is used to carry sick people to the hospital.
- Police van: A police van carries the police to different places to maintain law and order and also to help people in times of need.
- Fire engine: A fire engine is a special type of van that helps to put out fires.

Choosing the Mode of Travel

The choice of our mode of travel depends on two factors.

- The distance to be travelled. The cost of travel

People usually cover short distances using bicycles, rickshaws, tractors, boats, scooters, motorcycles, buses and cars. People use cars, buses, trains, trucks, aeroplanes and ships to cover long distances. For very long distances, people use ships, aeroplanes and trains. Rockets are used to travel to **outer space**: to go to the moon or to other planets.

We have to buy tickets to travel on aeroplanes, buses and trains. Air travel is the quickest and most expensive means of transport.

Fuel for Vehicles

Most vehicles need some **fuel** to move. Petrol, diesel and Compressed Natural Gas (CNG) are the most commonly used fuels.

Earlier, trains ran mostly on coal. Now, most trains and trams run on electricity. Cars and buses run on CNG, petrol and diesel. Aeroplanes run ona fuel that is specially made for them.

Burning fuel gives off fumes that can pollute the air. CNG creates less pollution than petrol and diesel. Vehicles like bicycles, cycle rickshaws, bullock carts and horse carts do not need any fuel and hence are pollution-free. We should try and use these vehicles to cover short distances.

My India

The toy train in Darjeeling is not just fun to ride, it also shows how smart people were to build it in the mountains. This train travels 83 km from Siliguri to Darjeeling and goes through beautiful hills. It is so special that it has been named a World Heritage Site. Why do you think building a train in the mountains was difficult? What makes the toy train in Darjeeling special compared to other trains?

The History of Transport

Early humans walked from place to place or rode on animals. They also used animals to transport things from place to place. Then they invented the wheel. The wheel was used with carts drawn by animals at first. Later on, many other vehicles such as bicycles, trains, scooters and cars were invented. All of these vehicles have wheels. The pictures show how the way people travel has changed over time. The invention of the wheel has been a very important event in the history of transport.

Early humans walked from place to place.

After the wheel was invented, it was used with carts drawn by animals.

Vehicles like bicycles were invented much later.

Modern vehicles like cars still use wheels.

Sustainable Development Goals (SDGs)

SDG 13: Climate Action

India has tested a new train that runs on hydrogen, a clean and green fuel. Unlike regular trains, it doesn't make smoke or pollute the air—it only gives out water! This helps keep our skies clear and our planet healthy. By using hydrogen, India is taking smart steps to fight climate change and protect nature. It is a great example of how science can help us care for the earth!

WAYS OF COMMUNICATION

The act of expressing our thoughts, feelings and ideas or sharing information with others is called communication. We communicate by talking or writing.

We communicate with others through different means of communication. In earlier times, people used sounds and signs to communicate. Slowly, some of these meaningful sounds, drumbeats and symbols became a **language**. There are many different languages that exist in the world today. Today, we can communicate with others by writing letters and by speaking on the telephone or mobile phone. We can also send messages through **mobile phones** or send emails through the internet. All these methods of sending and receiving messages are known as means of communication.

Broadly, means of communication are of two kinds:

1. Through one-to-one communication, we communicate with one person at a time.
2. Through mass communication, we communicate with many people at a time.

One-to-one Communication

Postal Communication

One of the most popular methods of communication is postal communication. The postal system helps us to send and receive letters. Writing letters helps people to keep in touch with one another, especially when they live far away from each other. We send and receive post through a post office. We can buy **stamps**, **postcards** and **inland letters** from the post office.

A letter box

Whenever we send a letter by post, we need to keep some important points in mind:

- We should write the address of the person to whom we are sending the letter clearly on the envelope. We should write the PIN code (Postal Index Number) along with the address. It ensures that the letter will reach the correct address. We should also write our own address on the back of the envelope.
- Stamps of different prices are used for different letters. The stamp that we should use depends on the place where we have to send a letter and the weight of that letter.
- We should put the letter in a letter box or give it at the post office for delivery.

Usually, a letter takes a few days to reach the person you are sending it to. If you want it to reach faster, you can use the Speed Post facility of the post office or other **courier services**. Both these services are costlier than the normal post. An aerogramme is used to send a letter to a person staying in another country. Post offices also have a facility called registered post through which very important documents can be sent.

Activity Corner

Write a short letter to your friend in class. Then, put it inside an envelope and stick a self-drawn stamp on it. Drop your envelope into our classroom post box. Tomorrow, our class postmaster will deliver the letters to the right desks!

Telephonic Communication

The telephone is the fastest means of communication. Through a telephone, we can talk to anyone living in any part of the world immediately.

Usually, telephone calls within our city cost less while calls to other parts of the country or the world cost more. Those who do not own a phone can use the phones in a PCO (Public Call Office) on paying a small amount of money. A fax machine helps us to send copies of documents instantly through a telephone line. We can only send documents by fax to someone who also has a fax machine.

Telephones have undergone changes over the years. Earlier we had telephones with wires. Now wireless and cordless phones are also available. Today, people use mobile phones or smart phones to talk to people or to send them **text messages** through SMS (Short Message Service) or through **social media** and **emails** which use an **internet** connection.

A smartphone

Communication through Computers

Today, people use computers to communicate with each other instantly. Messages or pictures can be sent through emails from one computer to another through the internet. People can also see and talk to each other through video conferencing through the internet. In order to communicate through computers, it is important that both the sender and the receiver have internet connections.

Fact Finder

Video conferencing was used a lot during covid times to continue studies at home. This helped in continuing education for schoolchildren. Find out the problems or challenges that one faced during this shift?

Mass Communication

There are many ways through which we can send messages to many people at once and at the same time. This is known as mass communication.

> **My Eco Club**
>
> Newspapers can be easily recycled to make many things like envelopes, paper bags, etc. Newspapers can also be used to make things made of papier mâché, which has been a craft since a long time in the region of Kashmir especially.

The different means of mass communication are newspapers, radio, television, and the internet. They are also known as mass media.

We have smart televisions nowadays.

A newspaper is a printed set of paper sheets that contains news and information about some important events happening in the world. Newspapers are printed in different languages.

A radio is an instrument that people use to listen to news and important information. We can also listen to songs and other programmes on the radio.

A television gives us information through sound and moving pictures. It is an effective means of mass communication.

The internet is another important means of mass communication. We can get all kinds of information from anywhere in the world at any time through the internet.

The means of communication have become faster and better over the years. We choose our means of communication based on our needs.

OCCUPATIONS IN TRANSPORT AND COMMUNICATION

A pilot

There are many different occupations that people do in the fields of transport and communication. A driver drives vehicles, while a mechanic fixes problems with vehicles. A conductor gives and checks tickets in buses and other public vehicles. A special person called a TTE (Travel Ticket Examiner) checks passengers for their valid tickets on trains. Similarly, most trains also have a guard and a driver.

A pilot flies an aeroplane. Most planes have air hostesses and air hosts that serve you while on flight. They make the journey as comfortable as possible for us. We should respect all jobs and show kindness towards all those who help us.

In the communications sector, a postman delivers letters, people like radio jockeys and TV anchors conduct programmes on the radio and TV for entertainment. News readers give us news of the world while journalists collect the news.

Our Values

Whatever means of communication we use, we should always be polite to people. We should always try to speak the truth and not hurt anyone.

- How do you think others would feel when we are rude to them?

Keywords

Vehicle: Anything that carries people or things from one place to another

Transport: A method of carrying people or things from one place to another

Outer space: The place far away outside the earth, where all the planets and starsare

Language: Words that people use to speak or write to each other

Mobile phone: A phone that you can carry around with you

Stamp: A small piece of paper that you put on a letter to show that you have paid to send it

Postcard: A card that you write on and send by post

Inland letter: A letter which can only be sent somewhere within the country

Courier service: A company that delivers important letters and parcels

Text message: A written message that you send using a mobile phone

Social media: Websites and software programs used for social networking

Email: A way of sending messages and data to other people by means of computers connected together in a network

Internet: A very large network of computers that are connected to each other

Let's Remember

Travel

- **Means of Transport**
  - Land—cycles, cars, trains, etc.
    Water—ships, yachts, etc.
    Air—aeroplanes, hot air balloons, etc.
  - Special vehicles—ambulance, police vans, etc.
- **Ways of Communication**
  - One-to-one: Postcards, letters,phonecalls, instant messaging
  - Mass: Radio, television, the internet, newspapers
  - Through language or writing
- **Occupations in Transport and Communication**
  - Pilots, driver, conductor, postman, TTE are some of the occupations.

Exercises

Remembering and Understanding

A. Choose the correct answers.

1. Which of these vehicles would help in case of a fire?
   (a) Train (b) Fire engine (c) Aeroplane (d) Ambulance
2. Which of these were used to communicate in earlier times?
   (a) Drumbeats (b) Smoke signals (c) Both of these (d) None of these
3. Which of these is not related to the postal service?
   (a) Stamps (b) Postcards (c) Speed Post (d) Email
4. Which of these is a means of one-to-one communication?
   (a) Letters (b) Radio (c) Television (d) None of these

B. Match the rows.

1. Cycle	2. Television	3. Tram	4. Stamp	5. Rockets
(a) Tracks	(b) Outer space	(c) Both pictures and sounds	(d) Short distances	(e) Postal communication

C. State whether true or false. Rewrite the false statements correctly.

1. Scooters and motorcycles are means of water transport.
2. Police van carries the sick to the hospital.
3. People can only communicate with each other on a one-to-one basis.
4. We can directly send and receive post without a postman or a post office.
5. We use a telephone to instantly communicate with people.
6. We can communicate through computers without an internet connection.

D. Answer the following questions.

1. What helps people choose the means of transport?
2. What are fuels? Name some commonly used fuels for transport.
3. What is communication? Mention any two ways in which people can communicate without speaking.
4. Write a short note on any three means of one-to-one communication.
5. Define mass communication. Write a brief note on any three means of mass communication.
6. Name three people who work on trains. Mention what each person does.

Reflect and Learn

21st CENTURY SKILLS

A. Discuss: Is it better for the environment to go to school in your own car every day or take the school bus instead? Why?

Communication

B. Think and Answer: Why should we write our own address at the back of the envelope when we are sending a letter to someone? Critical Thinking

C. The pictures here show the different means of communication. Number them in increasing order beginning from the oldest to the newest.

Project and Portfolio

21st CENTURY SKILLS

A. Individual: Collect pictures of means of land transport and paste them on a chart paper. Find out and write which ones are fast and which ones are slow, as well as the fuel each one runs on. C-6.2 SI Arts Education

B. Interdisciplinary: In small groups, enact a train journey or a scene at the railway station. Each group can take up different responsibilities of performing different tasks. C-6.1 SI Theatre

C. Field/Outdoor: Visit a local radio station or a local newspaper press and see how a radio broadcast is done, or how a newspaper is published. In groups of three, make a list of all the various activities that go into making a newspaper C-6.1

Self-review

Colour the smileys to show how well you have understood the concepts.	Completely	Mostly	Need help
• I can identify and differentiate between the different modes of transport of the present and the past.	☺	☺	☺
• I can explain means of communication at home/school/neighbourhood.	☺	☺	☺
• I can describe occupations in transport and communication.	☺	☺	☺

Teacher's Tip

Take the children for a visit to a post office and let them observe how the postal system works. Let them see the various kinds of postal services like inland letters, postcards, stamps, parcels, etc. You could also bring a radio to class and play it briefly. You can use your mobile phone to demonstrate text messaging and video conferencing.

16 Managing Our Wastes

Learning Outcomes

The learner:

- observes and identifies the different kinds of waste that get generated in our homes and communities.
- explains the importance of waste management.
- describes ways of conserving resources and managing resources well in daily life to live wisely.

Warm-up

Observe for a day and make a list of the different kinds of wastes that get generated every day at home.

In the Kitchen	In the Study Room	In the Garden	Wet Wastes

Circle all the wastes that can be reused in some way. C-4.7

All that is unwanted and gets generated in our day-to-day life is called **waste**.

TYPES OF WASTES

Different types of of wastes get created in different places while doing different activities.

Vegetable waste

These wastes can be grouped in many ways.

1. Dry wastes: Wastes like paper, cardboard envelopes, plastic, threads cloth etc can be placed here
2. Wet wastes: All food wastes and kitchen wastes, fruit and vegetable peels can be put in this
3. **Biodegradable** wastes: Wastes like food, paper, leaves, twigs, clay items, fruit and vegetable peels are biodegradable. They can be easily composted and converted into manure. They can be thrown into green dustbins.

4. Non-biodegradable wastes: Wastes like plastic bottles, metal items, rubber items, medicine strips, cans, glass items and plastic bags do not degrade and become manure. These items need to be managed better to reduce their harmful effects. They can be thrown into blue dustbins.

Dry waste

5. Recyclable wastes: Some wastes can be sent to special factories and **recycled** to make new products that can be used. Nowadays people recycle plastics, pieces of clothing, paper and other products to make new things.

Recyclable waste

Activity Corner

Sort the following wastes into the correct bin that you will throw in.

Medicine strip, clay pot, paper, cola can, glass bottle, plastic bottle, pencil, eraser, sharpener, dried leaves, twigs

C-4.7

Green Dustbin	Blue Dustbin

MANAGING WASTES

When garbage is not properly managed, it gets dumped here and there. This leads to plastic and other wastes thrown around. When cows and other animals try to eat plastic and other trash, they can fall sick.

It is very important to manage our wastes. Wastes when not managed well can be harmful to the environment and affect our health. It can also harm plant and animal life. Let us learn about waste management.

Controlling the Waste We Generate

We can reduce wastes that need to be disposed of by keeping the 3R's in mind and practising them.

My Eco Club

We must always carry cloth bags when we go shopping instead of plastic bags.

Reduce: When we start practicing steps to reduce waste generation, it helps in reducing the problem of removing wastes. We can do so in many ways:

1. While buying things, choose those which have less packaging.
2. Buy clothes that last a long time. When they do not fit, give them to someone else who can wear them.
3. Use things passed down from family or friends—like books, clothes, toys, and other items.
4. Use things that can be washed and used again, not things you throw away after one use.
5. Try not to buy too many new things. Get only what you need and help make less waste.

Reuse: When we practice reusing things, we can help in reducing the wastes that need to be managed. Mala's home reuses almost everything they can. Let us see how we can do so too.

We can reuse many things at home instead of throwing them away. Clean glass jars and bottles can store spices, milk, or water, and even be used as flower vases. Plastic containers from food can be used to store dals, nuts, or as small plant pots. Torn clothes can be used for cleaning or made into quilts and bags. Old newspapers and magazines can be used as wrapping paper. Plastic bags can be reused for shopping or as dustbin liners. Cardboard boxes are great for storing things or craft work. Metal cans can become pencil holders or planters. Egg cartons can help sort small items like buttons. Even old furniture can be redesigned and used again. Reusing things helps keep our homes and Earth clean!

My India

Waste to Wonder Park is a fun place in Delhi where you can see big models of the Seven Wonders of the World. These are made from old and waste materials! There's also a Dinosaur Park with moving dinosaurs made from scrap. It's a great place to learn how waste can be turned into something amazing! Can you name another famous example from Chandigarh?

Fact Finder

Nowadays Digital waste has also become a problem. Disposing off hardware equipment like an old monitor, CD ROMS, old CPU and even pen drives etc can lead to a lot of metallic wastes. Find out how big companies get rid of their digital wastes and discuss in class.

Recycle: Do you remember the *kabadiwalas* that visit our homes? In India we have been practicing recycling from generations. The *kabadiwala* sorts and takes discarded things from homes. These things are then sent to different factories, or repurpose them and make new things.

A kabadiwala taking old newspapers

When we recycle and use recycled things, we do not need to take too much from nature. It also helps keep our waste under control.

Be a Scientist

See how using recycled paper not just helps reduce wastes but also helps the environment in many ways.

- When we recycle paper and wood to make paper, need for virgin paper is reduced.
- Hence, fewer trees will be cut.
- When trees will not be cut for paper needs, forests and animals will not be harmed.
- Hence, the air will be cleaner.

Make a pictorial flowchart to show how using recycled paper helps the environment.

Think how wearing recycled clothes can help and write down five ways it can help the environment. C-6.2

Getting Rid of the Wastes Wisely

Find out how wastes get removed from home every day.

____

Have you ever wondered where these wastes go?

Besides recycling and reusing, wastes are generally managed through landfills and composting too.

Compost pit

In many cities, non-biodegradable wastes are dumped in pits called landfills. Over time these garbage dumps get packed and that land gets used as a park or even for housing on it. **Landfills** are a huge environment **hazard** because while the wastes are getting packed, they release harmful gases and poisonous chemicals in soil and air. This makes the area unfit for living.

Biodegradable wastes like the garden and kitchen wastes, on the other hand are usually composted. They are dumped in compost pits, where over time the wastes turn into manure, which can be used to make the soil fertile.

To manage wastes effectively, it is important to separate wastes. Hence the twin bin system is being promoted in many parts of India. Green dustbins are for wet waste like fruit peels, vegetable scraps, and leftover food. Blue dustbins are for dry waste like paper, plastic, glass, and metal. Wastes if not managed properly, can harm our environment and pollute the air, water and soil. This leads to harmful effects in the environment.

Sustainable Development Goals (SDGs)

Goal 15: Life on Land

In many Indian villages, people reuse things and create very little waste. They use vegetable peels for animals, carry cloth bags and turn old clothes into useful items. Cow dung is used for cooking and children share books and toys. This keeps their village clean, green and fresh!

Our Values

Instead of discarding old books, we should share them with our friends and others. We should use all diaries and notebooks till the end.

- Do you think it is wise to reuse things?
- Do you think it is wise to use second hand books instead of buying new ones. Why?

New Words

Wastes: Something that is no longer useful

Biodegradable: Natural wastes that can easily and naturally rot

Recycle: Process of making new things using existing things

Landfill: A large dumping ground that is filled with trash and compressed

Hazard: Something that can be dangerous or cause damage

Let's Remember

Managing Our Wastes

- **Types of Wastes** → Wastes can be dry, wet, biodegradable, non-biodegradable and recyclable.
- **Managing Wastes**
  - We need to control waste generation through the 3 Rs: Reduce, Recycle, Reuse
  - In general, waste is disposed of in landfills or through composting.
  - Green dustbins are for wet waste like fruit peels, vegetable scraps, and leftover food. Blue dustbins are for dry waste like paper, plastic, glass, and metal.

Exercises

A. Choose the correct answers. Remembering and Understanding

1. Which of the following can be recycled?
   (a) Glass jar (b) Plastic boxes (c) Newspapers (d) All of these
2. Which of the following is wet waste?
   (a) Food waste (b) Envelopes (c) Cloth (d) Cardboard
3. Which of these can be put in a compost pit?
   (a) Kitchen wastes (b) Plastic boxes (c) CDs (d) Glass bottles
4. Read the statements below and choose the correct option.
   Statement (A): Waste segregation cannot help in its management.
   Statement (B): Wastes need to be managed wisely.
   (a) Both (A) and (B) are true, and (B) is the correct explanation of (A).
   (b) Both (A) and (B) are true, but (B) is not the correct explanation of (A).
   (c) (A) is true but (B) is false. (d) (A) is false but (B) is true.

B. Write L for landfill and C for Composting to segregate where the wastes could go.

1. Fruit peels ________
2. Eggshells ________
3. Old shoe ________
4. Old T-shirt ________
5. Plastic bag ________
6. Cloth bag ________
7. Paper bag ________
8. Old pen ________
9. Disposable injection ________
10. Medicine strip ________

C. Give two examples for each of the following.

1. Biodegradable wastes ______________________________
2. Non-biodegradable wastes ______________________________
3. Recyclable things ______________________________
4. Methods of removing wastes ______________________________

D. Answer the following questions.

1. What are wastes? Give five ways in which wastes get generated at home.
2. What are the 3 R's? How would each of them help us in waste management?
3. Differentiate between Reusing and Recycling with an example
4. What is a landfill? How is it different from composting?
5. List five ways in which we can stay mindful and reduce waste generation at home.

Reflect and Learn

21st CENTURY SKILLS

A. Discuss: Is landfill a good method of managing wastes? Why? Communication

B. Think and Answer: Do you think by reducing packaging wastes we can reduce waste generation? Give reasons for your answer. Critical Thinking

C. **Read the text and answer the questions:** In many Indian towns and cities, we see women called *pheriwalis or bartan walis*. They go from house to house selling things or exchanging old items. A *bartan wali* often gives steel utensils in return for old clothes. These women carry their goods in baskets or on their heads and walk long distances every day. They help families reuse things and also earn money for their own homes. Their work is important in recycling of wastes.

1. Who are *pheriwalis or bartan walis*?
2. What do *bartan walis* give in exchange for old clothes?
3. How do these women carry their goods?
4. Why is their work important?

Project and Portfolio

21st Century Skills

A. Individual activity: Observe the wastes being generated in the kitchen of your home for a week and make a chart showing al the wastes generated with one suggestion on better management for each. (C-4.7, C-6.2) Observation

B. Group activity: In groups of five, create a compost pit using an old bucket or a pot, or a *ghada* and dump any ten kinds of wastes from home and observe what happens to each of them after a month. Prepare a report and share in class. (C-4.7) Collaboration

C. Interdisciplinary activity: Write a short imaginative story of the journey of a plastic bag dumped in a landfill. Share the challenges it would face and highlight the feelings of people living nearby. (C-6.2) SI English

Self-review

Colour the smileys to show how well you have understood the concepts.	Completely	Mostly	Need help
• I can observe and identify the different kinds of waste that get generated in our homes and communities.	☺	☺	☺
• I can explain the importance of waste management.	☺	☺	☺
• I can describe ways of conserving resources and managing resources well in daily life to live wisely.	☺	☺	☺

Teacher's Tip

Introduce the chapter by telling students the importance of keeping their surroundings clean. Tell them about the various waste management techniques through activities. Then discuss how we can all practise the 3 R's at home for effective waste management.

Problem Solving and Life Skills

Chapter 12

Prashant got a cotton and a plastic bag in a bowl of water for five minutes and then took them both out.

1. Which of the two bags would soak more water? ____________ (Cotton/ plastic)
2. If both these bags were kept in two different bowls, in which bowl would there be more water left behind?
   (a) Bowl with the Cotton bag
   (b) Bowl with the plastic bag
   (c) Both will have the same amount of water left
3. Which of the two would be better to use to stay dry?
   (a) Cotton because it soaks more water
   (b) Cotton because it soaks less water
   (b) Plastic because it soaks less or no water

Chapter 13

Bricks are most commonly made from clay. Clay is kneaded with water and then put in moulds to make bricks. They are then burnt in special places to get backed and become stronger.

1. Which of this is not true about bricks?
   (a) They are used to make strong houses
   (b) They are made from clay and baked
   c. They are used to make kutcha houses
2. Which of these would be needed to make bricks?
   (a) Clay, water and a place to bake
   (b) Clay and water only
   (c) Clay, water, mould and a place to bake

Chapter 14

1. Write the exact directions you would give to someone going from the bus stop to the bank.
2. Giving clear instructions is important for proper directions. Why? Give two reasons.

Chapter 15

Look at the picture and answer the questions below.

Observe the card that Yash wants to send to his grandmother living in Chennai.

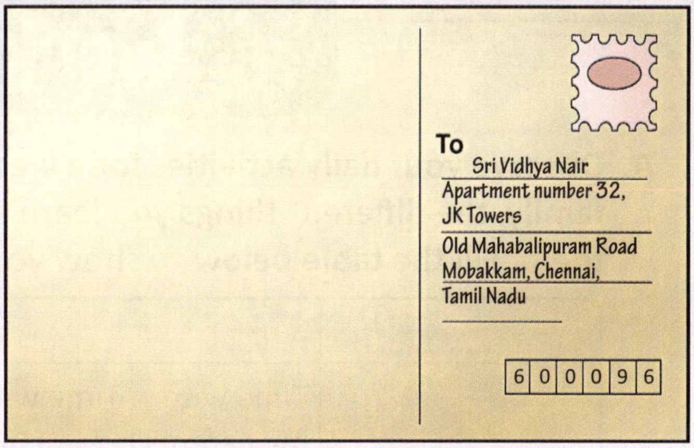

1. What do you think Yash is planning to use to send the card?

   (a) Email (b) Postal service (c) Telephone (d) Radio

2. What is the Pin code written here?
3. Which of these can be a fast mode of sending it?

   (a) Email (b) Fax (c) Courier service (d) Newspaper

Chapter 16

1. Look at the picture below. Are such dumping grounds a good way of disposing wastes? Give two reasons why.
2. How would such garbage dumps affect each of the following:

   (a) Soil ____________________

   (b) Water bodies ____________________

   (c) Air ____________________

3. How could wastes been thrown instead? Give two ways.

Worksheet 1

A. Observe your daily activities for a week. Note down all that you do with your family, the different things you learn about yourself and how you live life with them. Fill the table below to show your routine.

	My Family				
	Time with my parents	Time with my grandparents	What I learn about myself	Games I Play with my family	Who teaches me about life around?
Time (Weekdays)					
Time (Weekends)					
Activities I do/ What I eat (Weekdays)					
Activities I do/ What I eat (Weekends)					

B. Read the passage and answer the following questions.

Elephants have been a very important part in the lives of kings in olden times in India. Kings often gifted elephants to each other as a sign of their strength and richness. A lot of Indian paintings, buildings and even stories have elephants playing key roles. Elephant keepers and riders were called 'Mahouts' and it was considered a traditional occupation of people in olden times. These mahouts could talk to elephants and understand their body language, treat their diseases and help them stay healthy and fit. Today, mahouts are seen working in forest departments of many countries.

1. What made mahouts so special in India?
2. What could be two reasons why elephants were so popular in olden India and not so now?

   (a) ____________________

   (b) ____________________
3. Imagine yourself to be a mahout. What would your life be like? Draw pictures to show a day in your life as a mahout with your elephant.

Worksheet 2

Look at the picture and answer the questions that follow.

1. Is it better that the house has a sloping roof rather than a flat one? (Yes/ No) Justify your answer.
2. List a few ways in which she can use the collected rainwater
3. Which of these must have been used to make this utensil?

   (a) Clay (b) Sand and husk (c) Water (d) All of these
4. How come the woman is able to fill water easily in utensils of all shapes and sizes? Would it be possible to fit stones like that? Why?
5. Is this water fit for drinking?
6. How can she make it fit for drinking?
7. What would happen to the level of water if we leave a pot of water out in the sun for a few days? Explain why?

Sample Unit Test Paper I

Chapters: 1–4 **Time: 45 mins** **Marks: 25**

A. Choose the correct option. 3

1. Which of the following is true about a family tree?
   (a) People born around the same time belong to one generation.
   (b) Your grandparents are two generations older
   (c) You and your siblings belong to the same generation (d) All of these
2. Which of the following games can be played both indoors and outdoors?
   (a) Carrom ☐ (b) Basketball ☐ (c) Football ☐ (d) Kho-kho ☐
3. Which of the following is a long-unstitched cloth used by women to cover their heads?
   (a) Frog ☐ (b) Toad ☐ (c) Both of these ☐ (d) None of these ☐

B. Fill in the blanks with the correct words. 3

1. We meet our ___________ (joint/extended) relatives when there is a celebration in the family.
2. Many __________ (tableaux/posters) showcase the culture of states during Republic Day.
3. Some indoor games are ludo, chess, carrom and other _________(board/court) games.

C. State whether true or false. 3

1. Our father's parents are our maternal grandparents.
2. A mela builds culture and traditions.
3. Chhath Puja is an important festival celebrated in Maharashtra.

D. Read the riddle on the right and answer the questions below. 8

> I bloom in pink, a lovely sight, In Shillong's hills, I shine so bright. November's breeze brings songs and cheer, With dances, music, and joy so near. Guess my name, I'm nature's call—A festival loved by one and all!

1. Which festival is being described?
   (a) Mango Festival (b) Rose Festival (c) Cherry Blossom Festival (d) Tulip Festival
2. In which month does it take place?
   (a) January (b) March (c) November (d) July
3. What flower is the highlight of this festival?
   (a) Rose (b) Sunflower
   (c) Cherry blossom (d) Lotus
4. What kind of events are held during this festival?
   (a) Sports matches (b) Cultural programs (c) Science exhibitions (d) Cooking contests

E. Look at the picture and answer the following questions. 4

1. Which game is shown here?
   (a) Tennis (b) Carom (c) Cricket (d) Ludo
2. Which kind of game is it?
   (a) Indoor (b) Outdoor (c) Watersport (d) Card game
3. What type of game is it?
   (a) Racket game (b) Card game
   (c) Board game (d) Video game

F. Answer the following questions. 4

1. Explain the similarities between family members.
2. How does a mela play an important role?

Sample Unit Test Paper 2

Chapters: 5–8 **Time: 45 mins** **Marks: 25**

A. Choose the correct option. 3

1. Which of the following do women wear in Assam?
   (a) Pheran ☐ (b) Mekhla ☐ (c) Pagri ☐ (d) Salwar-kameez ☐
2. Which of the following is not a herb?
   (a) Mint ☐ (b) Spinach ☐ (c) Cotton ☐ (d) Coriander ☐
3. Which of the following is a domestic animal?
   (a) Donkey ☐ (b) Porcupine ☐ (c) Tiger ☐ (d) Whale ☐

B. Fill in the blanks with the correct words. 3

1. Animals that eat only plants are called ____________(herbivores/carnivores).
2. The __________(beak/claw) of a bird helps catch food and make a nest.
3. __________(Earthworms/snails) help to make the soil more fertile by turning and loosening it.

C. State whether true or false. 3

1. A salwar kurta is an unstitched garment set.
2. Stems are known as the kitchen of a plant.
3. Tigers and panthers are carnivores.

D. Read the poem on the right and answer the questions below. 8

I bloom from a bud, a colourful sight, I help plants grow with nature's might. Some love my scent, some seek my hue, And buzzing friends help me bear fruit too.

1. Identify what is being talked about in the passage.
   (a) Roots (b) Flowers (c) Leaves (d) Seeds
2. How do they help plants multiply?
   (a) By storing food (b) By absorbing sunlight
   (c) By turning into fruits with seeds
   (d) By growing taller
3. From where do they grow?
   (a) From a seed (b) From a leaf (c) From a bud (d) From a root
4. Which of the following can be used to make perfumes?
   (a) Rose (b) Jasmine (c) Sweet pea (d) All of these

E. Look at the picture and answer the following questions. 4

1. Which species of animal is shown here?
   (a) Reptiles (b) Birds (c) Insect (d) Fish
2. Which part of the body do they use to feel the world around them?
3. How many legs does this animal usually have?

F. Answer the following questions. 4

1. Draw and label the parts of a bird's body.
2. Mention four ways in which plants are useful to us.

Sample Unit Test Paper 3

Chapters: 9–12 **Time: 45 mins** **Marks: 25**

A. Choose the correct option. **3**

1. Which festival is associated with river and water bodies?
   (a) Baisakhi ☐ (b) Diwali ☐ (c) Chhath Puja ☐ (d) Bihu ☐
2. Which of the following is not a body-building food?
   (a) Eggs ☐ (b) Meat ☐ (c) Milk ☐ (d) Wheat ☐
3. Which of the following is a special vehicle which takes the sick to a hospital?
   (a) Crane ☐ (b) Jeep ☐ (c) Ambulance ☐ (d) Motorcycle ☐

B. Fill in the blanks with the correct words. **3**

1. The immediate help given to an injured person is called______________ (first aid/bandage)
2. Things that allow you to see through them are called _________ (transparent/opaque) things.
3. Solids have a ___________ (fixed/loose) shape and size.

C. State whether true or false. **3**

1. Water found under the ground is known as groundwater.
2. Animals like cows, buffaloes and goats give us wool.
3. A bad touch feels nice and safe.

D. Read the passage and answer the questions below. **8**

Sometimes, we may get into an emergency even when we are careful. We or someone else may either get hurt or there could be a fire breakout. In case of fire, we should immediately call 101 and alert the nearest fire station. There are many causes for fire. Sometimes a fire is caused due to an electrical fault. In that case we should never try to put out that fire, using water. Such fires can be put out using sand or special instruments called fire extinguishers. We should never play with fire.

1. Identify what kind of situation is being described in the passage.
   (a) A picnic plan (b) A school event (c) An emergency situation (d) A gardening activity
2. How should one respond in case of a fire breakout?
   (a) Call 100 and wait for help (b) Try to put out the fire with water
   (c) Call 101 and alert the nearest fire station (d) Run away without informing anyone
3. From where an electrical fire can be safely put out?
   (a) Using water (b) Using sand or fire extinguishers
   (c) Using a cloth (d) By switching off the fan
4. Which of the following is a safety rule mentioned in the passage?
   (a) Always keep water nearby (b) Never play with fire
   (c) Use candles during power cuts (d) Keep windows closed during fire

E. Look at the picture and answer the following questions. **4**

1. Which natural process is shown in the picture?
2. What does this help circulate?
   (a) Clouds (b) Droplets (c) Water (d) Air
3. From the picture, explain the process briefly.

F. Answer the following questions. **4**

1. What are the main types of foods? Give two examples of each.
2. Differentiate between a solid, liquid and a gas with two examples of each.

Sample Unit Test Paper 4

Chapters: 13–16 | **Time: 45 mins** | **Marks: 25**

A. Choose the correct option. 3

1. Which of the following is not used to make pucca houses?
   (a) Straw ☐ (b) Cement ☐ (c) Steel ☐ (d) Mortar ☐
2. What is the rough drawing of a place called?
   (a) Map ☐ (b) Landmark ☐ (c) Scale ☐ (d) Sketch ☐
3. Which of the following can you buy from a post office?
   (a) Stamps ☐ (b) Postcards ☐ (c) Inland letters ☐ (d) All of these ☐

B. Fill in the blanks with the correct words. 3

1. ___________ (Glazing/Baking) means covering pottery with a special liquid before baking it.
2. Most vehicles need some _____________ (fuel/water) to move.
3. It is very important to ___________ (manage/dump) our wastes.

C. State whether true or false. 3

1. Knitting is the process of colouring the cloth by soaking it in a coloured solution.
2. A fire engine is a special type of van that helps to put out fires.
3. Landfills are a huge environment hazard.

D. Read the riddle on the right and answer the questions below. 4

This shows you the lay of the land,
So you know where things can be found.
Many of them also show roads,
So you know how to get around.

1. Identify the item from the riddle.
   (a) Cars (b) Pots (c) Maps (d) none of these
2. What colours are used to represent its different features?
   (a) Brown (b) Blue (c) Green (d) all of these
3. Which of the following is usually at the bottom of this item?
   (a) north (b) south (c) west (d) east
4. Who among the following uses this item?
   (a) pilots (b) sailors (c) both of these (d) none of these

E. Look at the picture and answer the questions below. 4

1. What is being done in the picture?
2. Is it good for the environment? Why or why not?
3. What can be done instead?
4. What is the green and blue dustbin system?

F. Answer the following questions. 8

1. Write a short note on how to draw a map.
2. Explain the 3 Rs: Reduce, reuse and recycling.

Holistic Progress Card

Name: ________________ Class: ________________ Roll no: ________________ Year: ________________

Review your progress by marking a tick (✓) in the appropriate column. Your partner and teacher can mark their responses in the respective columns.

Competencies	Self-Review		Peer Review		Teacher Review	
	I can do.	I can improve.	Can do	Can improve	Can do	Can improve
C-1.1: Observes and identifies the natural (insects, plants, birds, animals, geographical features, sun and moon, stars, planets, natural resources) and social (houses, relationships) components in their immediate environment						
C-1.2: Describes relationships (including between humans and animals/nature) and traditions (art forms, celebrations, festivals) in the family and community						
C-1.3: Asks questions and makes predictions about simple patterns (season change, food chain, phases of the moon, movement of stars and planets, shapes of trees, plants, leaves, and flowers, rituals, celebrations) observed in the immediate environment						
C-1.4 Explains the functioning of local institutions (family, school, bank/post office, market, and panchayat) in different forms (story, drawing, tabulating data, reports), and analyses their roles						
C-1.5: Uses local materials to create simple objects (family tree, envelopes, origami animals) on their own for display or use in classroom processes						
C-2.1: Identifies natural and humanmade systems that support their lives (water supply, water cycle, river flow systems, seasons, life cycle of plants and animals, food, household items, transport, communication, electricity in the home)						
C-2.3: Connects changes in the environment and the lives of their family and community, as communicated by elders and through local stories (changes in occupation, food habits, resources, celebrations, communication)						
C-3.1: Describes the basic safety needs and protection (health and hygiene, food, water, shelter, precautions, awareness of emergency situations, abuse, and unsafe situations) of humans, birds, and animals						
C-3.3: Develops simple labels and slogans, and participates in roleplay on safety and protection in the local environment to be displayed/done in school and locality						
C-4.1: Observes and describes diversity among plants, and birds and animals in their immediate environment (shape, sounds, food habits, growth, habitat)						
C-4.4: Demonstrates how natural resources can be shared, maintained, and conserved (trees, use of rainwater, benefits of millets)						
C-4.5: Identifies needs of plants, birds, and animals, and how they can be supported (water, soil, food, care)						
C-4.7: Learns about basic social and behavioural norms, values, and dispositions that benefit our social and natural environments and that help our society function smoothly (using dustbins, standing in queues, conserving water, using public transportation, keeping one's environment clean, always helping others in need regardless of background)						
C-5.2: Draws a sketch of their school, village, and ward using symbols and directions						
C-5.3: Reads simple maps of city, state, and country to identify natural and humanmade features (well, lake, post office, school, hospital) with reference to symbols and directions						
C-6.1: Performs simple inquiry related to specific questions independently or in groups						
C-6.2: Presents observations and findings through different creative modes (drawing, diagram, poem, play, skit, oral and written expression)						
C-7.1: Gains familiarity with using the scientific method in investigations, as well as familiarity with other crosscutting concepts such as energy, matter, and systems that apply across the domains of science and engineering						
C-7.2: Gains familiarity with disciplinary core ideas in the natural sciences, as well as in engineering, technology, and applications of science, which reflect the content that will be learned across subject areas in later Grades						